Great AND ~~Horrible~~
— NEW~~S~~

BLESSIN ADAMS

In early modern Britain, murder truly was most foul. Trials were gossipy events packed to the rafters with noisome spectators. Executions were public proceedings which promised not only gore, but desperate confessions and the grandest, most righteous human drama. Grisly stories of crime and death sold like hot cakes.

This history unfolds the true stories of murder, criminal investigation, early forensic techniques, high court trials and so much more.

In a thrilling narrative, we follow a fugitive killer through the streets of London, citizen detectives clamouring to help officials close the net. We untangle the mystery of a suspected staged suicide through a newly emerging science of forensic pathology. We see a mother trying to clear her dead daughter's name while other women faced accusations – sometimes true and sometimes not – of murdering their own children.

These stories are pieced together from original research using coroner's inquests, court records, parish archives, letters, diaries and the cheap street pamphlets that proliferated to satisfy a voracious public.

These intensely personal stories portray the lives of real people as they confronted the extraordinary crises of murder, infanticide, miscarriage and suicide. Many historical laws and attitudes concerning death and murder may strike us as exceptionally cruel, and yet many remind us that some things never change: we are still fascinated by narratives of murder and true crime, murder trials today continue to be grand public spectacles, female killers are frequently cast as aberrant objects of public hatred and sexual desire, and suicide remains a sin within many religious organisations and was a crime in Britain until the 1960s.

Great and Horrible News explores the strange history of death and murder in early modern England, yet the stories within may appear shockingly familiar.

@WMCOLLINSBOOKS | WILLIAMCOLLINSBOOKS.COM

Great
AND
Horrible
NEWS

STORIES OF MURDER

AND MAYHEM IN

EARLY MODERN BRITAIN

BLESSIN
ADAMS

WILLIAM
COLLINS

William Collins
An imprint of HarperCollins*Publishers*
1 London Bridge Street
London SE1 9GF

WilliamCollinsBooks.com

HarperCollins*Publishers*
1st Floor, Watermarque Building, Ringsend Road
Dublin 4, Ireland

First published in Great Britain in 2023 by William Collins

1

Copyright © Blessin Adams 2023

Blessin Adams asserts the moral right to be identified as the author of this work
in accordance with the Copyright, Designs and Patents Act 1988

A catalogue record for this book is available from the British Library

ISBN 978-0-00-850022-1

Typeset in Minion Pro by
Palimpsest Book Production Ltd, Falkirk, Stirlingshire

Printed and bound in the UK using 100% renewable electricity at
CPI Group (UK) Ltd

This book is produced from independently certified FSC™ paper

to ensure responsible forest management.

For more information visit: www.harpercollins.co.uk/green

In loving memory of my father,
David Dixon.
This is for you Dad.

CONTENTS

GREAT AND
HORRIBLE NEWS

There was a great deal of excitement in the city of York in 1689. The newly raised regiment of the Duke of Bolton and Lord Castleton's Regiment of Foot were quartered there, and from London came heaving wagon loads of clothes, stores and supplies necessary to transform them from raw recruits to ready fighting men. The citizens of York looked upon the regiments as both a blessing and a curse; with the arrival of so many men there was money to be made, but inevitably there was also trouble to be had. Drunkenness, brawling and other foolish misdemeanours were expected but certainly not tolerated, and any soldier up to no good was hauled to the main guard and slung into a prison cell to cool his heels. This was the fate of an ex-butcher who had recently signed up with the regiment. He had committed some petty offence and as a result was locked up alone inside a prison cell. For reasons understood by nobody but himself, the new recruit stripped himself naked and, using a butcher's knife he had hidden on his person, 'ript himself from the hollow of his stomach to his navel' before reaching inside the hot cavity of the wound to pull out his own guts. Taking up his knife once again, he chopped his intestines into eight or ten pieces and threw them upon the floor, before finally collapsing in a pool of his own viscera.

When the guards came to check on their prisoner they were horrified to discover the gory scene inside the cell. To their further amazement they found that the soldier was still alive and cognisant of his surroundings. This strange and violent act of self-mutilation was unlike anything the people of York had ever seen before, and they flocked to the prison cell in droves to stare in wonder at the soldier as he lay dying. Spectators filed in and out of the cell like passing visitors at a country fair, with upwards of forty people at a time crammed shoulder-to-shoulder around the suffering man. After several hours the soldier stunned his audience by heaving himself upright and crawling into a chair, where he sat for an agonising nine hours before he finally died. Those lucky enough to have got a glimpse of this macabre scene were quick to relate it to their friends and families. The wagon masters visiting from London took the news of the soldier's suicide back to the capital, and before long the printing presses were running at full speed to push the story out to a public eager to snap up true-crime stories of bloody murder and suicide.

'Great and horrible news', thundered pamphlet headlines, which promised to give their readers 'a full relation of a person who rip'd his guts open and cut them in pieces'. The early moderns were obsessed by stories of death, crime and justice and they consumed true-crime narratives through a wide range of media, including but not limited to pamphlets, newspapers, court transcripts, sermons, broadside ballads, songs and drama. The public thrilled to read stories of dastardly highwaymen, executions, conmen, rogues, vagabonds and murderers. Booksellers lined their stalls with those small, unbound booklets that were typically only a few pages long and fronted by emotionally charged headlines and eye-grabbing woodcut illustrations depicting bloody and violent acts. These pamphlets were especially popular among the middling and upper literate classes, who deemed their reading material to be perfectly respectable fare. Semi-literate and illiterate fans of true crime enjoyed the drama of broadside ballads in single-sheet publications in which tales of true crime were written in the form of songs set to popular tunes. It was not unusual for inns and alehouses to cover their walls with true-crime broadside ballad sheets, ready and waiting for any semi-literate drinkers, who so wished, to entertain and inform their fellow patrons with the latest murder news.

True crime was popular not only because it titillated audiences with exceedingly gruesome tales, it also provoked in its readers powerful emotional responses and no small measure of moral outrage. Reading about shocking crimes and exercising one's indignation has long been a popular pastime. True-crime publications were more than news sheets describing the details of murder; they also sought to provide moral and religious instruction along with occasional, practical advice to fearful citizens who were keen to avoid becoming victims of crime themselves. More than anything, however, the early moderns were drawn to true-crime narratives because they touched upon fears tucked away in the darkest corners of their hearts: these are dreadful events that happen to other people, may they never happen to us.

The true tales of murder that feature in this book cover a period of some 200 years, from approximately 1500 to 1700. It was a time that encompassed the rise and fall of the Houses of the Tudors and the Stuarts, the English Civil War, the Protectorate, the Restoration and the Glorious Revolution. England split from Rome, and the country was torn asunder by the Protestant Reformation and Counter-Reformations. Medieval superstitions began to wane, and secular knowledge flourished through movements such as the Renaissance, the Enlightenment and the Scientific Revolution. Through these centuries countless wars were waged, plagues ebbed and flowed, the countryside was transformed by enclosure and cities and urban populations grew exponentially. The lives of individual men and women were shaped, sometimes irrevocably so, by the significant events of their time. Yet, first and foremost, this is a book that is interested in the personal, human experiences of everyday people as they confronted death in its most extreme, violent and tragic forms. Through the surviving historical records we can step into crime scenes from hundreds of years ago, examine clues and objects left behind, and hear the voices of victims, families, witnesses and perpetrators as they navigated the crises that had devastated their lives.

As an ex-police officer I found the experience of exploring historical records of crime and murder to be strangely familiar. In my old profession I often stood upon the threshold of scenes of sudden, violent and unnatural deaths. Walking into those scenes, I felt myself passing from the role of spectator to active player in the story of a complete stranger's death. They would never know me, but perhaps I would come to discover a little about them as I entered into their private space, touched their personal effects and inspected their body. On the whole I examined scenes of sudden death through the lens of professional training, but I couldn't help be moved on a personal level by the remaining artefacts of an everyday life now gone: an unfinished paperback novel on the bedside table, last night's dishes waiting to be washed up, or a well-worn pair of shoes with the backs flattened by years of hurried use. It was not only the mystery of sudden death that fascinated me, but all the details of life that remained in its wake. Just such artefacts are also present in historical records, and while we shall never know the people written about in those documents we nonetheless can be moved by the small details of their lives that remain after death.

The Bow Street Runners, founded in 1749, are often credited as the first professional police force in Britain. This did not mean that prior to the eighteenth century Britain was a lawless land. From the Middle Ages there existed a number of sophisticated law enforcement agencies and courts that maintained law and order, investigated crimes and punished criminals. Justices of the peace had the power to investigate felony offences, question suspects and witnesses, keep the peace and bind over troublemakers. Sheriffs and their under-officers worked locally to uphold the laws, keep the streets safe, conduct arrests, manage gaols, serve writs and ensure the smooth running of the courts. Coroners investigated all unnatural and suspicious deaths and could imprison suspects, take depositions, seize property and seek out fugitives in their quest to discover the cause of death. Citizens also played a far more active part in law enforcement in the roles of constables and high-constables, whose duties encompassed liaising on behalf of the local parishioners with the higher legal powers, and presenting all 'bloodshedds, assaltes, affreyes and outcryes' to the relevant authorities. Under the direction of the constables every household within a parish was expected to take its turn serving on the night watch, to patrol the streets, keep their neighbours safe and stamp out criminal activity.

While the mechanisms of law enforcement in the early modern period were ancient, the methods by which murder was investigated were slowly changing, innovating and modernising. Forensic pathology and toxicology were newly emerging sciences, and surgeons, physicians and coroners alike sought not only to identify but to classify the symptoms of death. This was the era that ushered in the Enlightenment and the Scientific Revolution; it was a time of rational thought in which professionals in secular fields held evidence as being superior to belief. It was no small wonder that revolutions of thought in the worlds of science and medicine were to filter down on to the front line of criminal investigation. Some coroners strove to establish logical methodologies as they processed crime scenes, gathered material evidence, examined bodies and questioned witnesses. Those men in the business of law and justice in the early modern period combined good old-fashioned detective work with the innovative ideas coming out of the schools of science and medicine. The way in which early modern investigators approached potential crime scenes may strike readers today as being not only forward-thinking but decidedly modern. Yet progress was a slow process, and many professional bodies were resistant to change. By and large the investigation of murder in the sixteenth and seventeenth centuries was intuitive, and successful prosecutions often came down to the intelligence and experience of individual investigators.

Those men who worked to untangle the mysteries of sudden and violent death were often driven by a need to see justice done. It was said that the common laws of England were born of an innate spirit of justice that lived in the hearts of all men. For many prominent legal writers the process of law was above all things a force of moral goodness that was essential to the common well-being of all. Yet not all citizens in early modern England were protected by those laws. Indeed, for many the laws of the land seemed by their very nature to be cruel, immoral and unjust. Women in particular suffered under legal systems that were ostensibly designed to protect them, but in truth worked to oppress them. Women could rarely expect any independence outside the rule of men and they were daily managed by laws that sought to control almost every aspect of their lives. This was considered to be the natural order of things. When women committed murder, in particular when women killed children, it seemed that nobody quite knew what to make of them. Their actions not only transgressed criminal law, they transgressed natural law. Such women were recast as un-women, monstrous beings whose perverse natures required punishment that was as much vengeance as it was due process. In their zeal to punish the so-called unnatural crimes of women, legislators undermined the principle in English law of the presumption of innocence as they forced those delivered of dead infants to prove that they had not murdered their own children.

The definition of murder in early modern England was broader than it is today. Suicide was understood to be a species of self-murder, and the law bizarrely sought to punish those who had killed themselves even though they were already dead. Coroners investigated suicides as though they were homicides, and treated the corpse of the dead as being both victim and perpetrator. Those found guilty of self-murder were subjected to ritualised acts of mutilation and profane burial which signified their excommunication from the Church. Furthermore, their families were also punished by laws which looked to strip them of their inheritance and force them into poverty. Self-murder was utterly reviled by the early modern public as both a spiritual and secular crime, and never before in English legal history had suicide been persecuted with such enthusiastic hostility. Yet this was a period in which the religious superstitions of the Middle Ages were gradually losing their hold upon the public imagination and lay people were beginning to understand suicide as a medical and social issue as well as a criminal one. Attitudes were painfully slow to change, however by the end of the seventeenth century the public had a greater capacity to feel sympathy, and perhaps even understanding, towards those who had been found guilty of murdering themselves. Many of the attitudes expressed by the early moderns towards suicides may seem incredibly harsh; however we must remember that such views were not just a relic of a long-distant past. Suicide was not decriminalised in England until 1961, and the Church of England did not permit full funerals for suicides until 2015.

Stories of murder and mayhem in early modern England often come to us in a piecemeal fashion through print and manuscript records that are fragmentary and faded by time. My research is drawn from a wide range of sources, which include coroners' inquest records, court documents, pamphlets, newspaper articles, ballads, wills, letters and diaries. Within these records we find fascinating, disturbing and often deeply moving tales of murder as told by those who were personally involved or who bore witness to those events. The stories in this book are true, yet we must remember that they were presented and recorded by individuals and groups who had their own biases, motivations and agendas. Nonetheless, I believe it is important to preserve the voices of the dead, and so when quoting from these sources I have expanded the trickier contractions but otherwise kept the original spelling. One of the agonies in researching crime in this period is that so much of the historical record has not survived. Many records have simply been lost or destroyed, others thrown away in the name of bureaucratic efficiency, a few have been stolen, and many yet remain undiscovered in the dark recesses of archives and libraries. From what small pieces we have, there are to be found amazing stories of the lives and deaths of people that at once seem so distant and yet so familiar.

MURDER ON
MILK STREET

In the summer of 1657, it was said that to be in Cheapside was to be in the heart of commercial luxury in London. Running over 300 yards long and almost 20 yards wide, Cheapside was easily one of the largest and brightest open areas within the city. This broad thoroughfare was the ideal location for grand public events: crowds could gather for markets, pageants, announcements and executions. Cheapside was at once a bustling commercial district and a residential area. Each side of the street was tightly lined with rows of magnificent timber-framed stone houses which often towered up to four or five storeys high. These properties were among the fairest and most exclusive in the city. Wealthy merchants called Cheapside home, and the ground-floor spaces of their expensive street-side properties served as shops, from which they displayed a dazzling array of goods. Browsing customers were guided by an eclectic arrangement of shop signs suspended by brackets that extended out over the street: suns and moons, animals and mythical beasts, body parts and everyday objects served as visual enticements for the services and goods to be found within. The accumulative noise of brisk trade and industry that drifted from the shops, courtyards and warehouses of Cheapside created an atmosphere that was both exciting and alive.

The west end of Cheapside was inhabited by the goldsmiths, whose displays of gold plate, silver, pearls and jewels greatly enhanced the 'bewtie and glorie' of the street. In addition to their eye-catching shopfronts, the goldsmiths dressed their wives in their finest wears and seated them outside to act as living advertisements. These women, passing lazy summer days draped in the height of fashion and bedecked in sumptuous jewels, piqued the envy of ladies who aspired to be as beautiful and as seemingly carefree. The east end of Cheapside was largely occupied by textile merchants, tailors, haberdashers and cloth-workers. These tradesmen boasted the finest textiles in all London, offering rich velvets, silks and satins, which according to one amazed observer were measured in lengths of the street's whole breadth. Here one could purchase clothes as well as cloth, from hoods, broad-brimmed hats, capes and caps to fine silk buttons, purses and ribbons. Slashed sleeves, full skirts, lace, trim collars and long coats were *de rigueur*, and the daring new craze for cravats was starting to take hold. If one desired the best of the best, then Cheapside was the place to be.

Branching off from Cheapside were the many side streets and lanes named after the medieval markets that once thrived there. Milk Street, Bread Street, Fish Street and Honey Lane no longer offered the goods specific to their namesakes, but they were nonetheless busy hives of commercial activity. Indentured apprentices and servants raced through those streets as they went about their master's business: they looked after shops, kept the books, produced wares and portered goods. When not hard-pressed with work, these servants carved out their spare time in the many taverns and alehouses lining the side streets and back alleys. The Mermaid inn, the Maidenhead, the Panier and the King's Head each boasted the finest liquid refreshments and victuals in town. The merry and drunk alighting from these back-alley pubs wound their way home along warrens that were confined on each side by tall merchant houses. Gabled upper storeys jutted outwards, encroaching into the sky and enclosing all below within a perpetual gloom. While the *crème de le crème* of London society promenaded through the bright, open space of Cheapside, the countless souls who serviced their needs ran their errands through the shady, yet nonetheless prosperous, side streets.

Many of the young apprentices working in and around Cheapside had come into the city from the surrounding counties in the hope of making better lives for themselves. The parents of young boys bound their sons by legal contract into indentured apprenticeships, sending them away to live and work in the capital for a period of up to ten years. This was not heartlessly done: parents who sent their children away did so with the intention of securing for them stable and successful lives. In London they could learn a trade and make connections that would ensure their future and those of their families. This was the fate of a young and timid-natured boy from Berkshire named John Knight. When he was seventeen years old John was sent to London to enter into the service of Mr Worth, a 'silk man' or silk merchant whose shop was situated at the south end of Milk Street, in view of the hustle and bustle of Cheapside. To be translated from the rural ideal of Berkshire into the beating heart of commercial London must have been an exhilarating and frightening experience.

John was in many respects an extremely lucky young man, for Mr Worth was a respectable merchant and his premises on Milk Street were situated among the finest establishments in the whole of London. John Stow, in his 1598 *Survey of London*, described Milk Street as containing 'many fair houses for wealthy merchants' and other notable citizens. The famous lawyer and humanist Sir Thomas More was born to an eminently respectable couple on Milk Street and he spent his youth passing to and fro along the busy side streets of Cheapside. At the south end of Milk Street, situated on the corner with the main thoroughfare of Cheapside, was the church of St Mary Magdalen. Here young John Knight would have attended the regular Sunday service, and perhaps whiled away those hours gazing upon the memorials of several of the city's past mayors. To the north end of the street was situated a 'fair well with two buckets' that was later converted into a well pump. Milk street and its immediate environs were, on the whole a handsome, safe and prosperous place for John to live and train in his new profession.

It was fortunate that John's parents were able to secure him a position at Mr Worth's silk shop, for silk men were an elite mercantile group who were ranked among the wealthiest in all London. Not just anybody could become a silk man. It was widely know, and resented, that it required a great deal of capital to establish oneself in the silk trade. Indeed, it was easier to set up in banking than in silk. Even more fortuitous for John was that his master was, by all accounts, a fair and kind man. John clearly thrived in his new role. He excelled in his training and over a two-year period had worked himself into a position of trust whereby he was tasked with running the silk shop while Mr Worth was out of London on business. This responsibility was a great honour, but since he was a timid young man it was not one that John relished. On the contrary, he confessed to his friends that when Mr Worth left the city he became fearful and hated to be left alone in the shop, especially at night, when the darkness amplified his dread and turned every small sound into the footsteps of thieves and villains.

In July 1657 Mr Worth announced to his young apprentice that he would be going away on business to Bristol Fair for several weeks, leaving John in sole charge. The heavy keys to the shop were handed over, and instructions given for John to keep a keen eye on both the business and the maidservants who slept on the top floor. It wasn't long after his master had departed that John became consumed with anxiety. Unable to cope with the prospect of sleeping alone, John begged his friend Nathaniel Butler to stay with him as his bedfellow during the nights his master was away. Such an arrangement might hint at a homosexual relationship between John and Nathaniel, although it must be noted that communal sleeping between men, even strangers at roadside inns, was a commonplace and entirely platonic practice in this period. Lack of censure in any surviving records, at a time when such censure would have been almost certain, suggests that their relationship was most likely simply one of friendship.

Nathaniel hailed from the market town of Alton in Hampshire, and was an apprentice to Mr Goodday, a 'drawer of cloth' with a shop on Carter Street, near St Paul's. Unlike John, Nathaniel was not a model employee. He had been 'turned over', essentially sacked, by his two previous masters, who could not wait to be rid of their unruly and feckless young apprentice. His contract of service had been signed over to anybody who would suffer to take him. It is not known how old Nathaniel was in the summer of 1657, however by law an apprentice could be no older than twenty-four. Since he had already been in service to two previous masters, he was likely to have been in his late teens or early twenties. Nathaniel was by his own admission a lazy and deceitful youth who frequently sold goods stolen from Mr Goodday to fund his addiction to gambling, drink and 'harlots'. He delighted in running with a bad crowd and claimed to have turned several of his more impressionable friends to the art of 'cozening', cheating and stealing. Perhaps the mild-natured John was impressed by this older companion, who seemed to navigate life with a self-assurance that was in equal parts grounded in arrogance and grit. John's parents had hoped that the course of their son's life was to be guided by the honest hand of Mr Worth; however they had no power in choosing his friends.

John and Nathaniel slept together for fourteen days while

Mr Worth was away in Bristol. During that time they ensured their arrangement was kept a secret. This was easily done, as John was almost always the first to rise in the mornings and the last to retire at night. Over the past few weeks it had become his habit to sneak Nathaniel in and out of the shop while the maidservants were asleep. On Tuesday, 4 August the two young apprentices were going through their usual late-night routine. John discreetly let Nathaniel inside the shop via the back door, and while he closed up the business Nathaniel stood idly by combing his hair. Using the keys entrusted to him by Mr Worth, John opened the shop's till to inspect several bags of money that were secured within. The ever-watchful Nathaniel peered over John's shoulder and fixed his greedy eyes upon those bags. Such a fortune was irresistible to a seasoned thief whose previous opportunities had amounted to no more than small drabs of change. As the luxuries afforded by such wealth played through Nathaniel's imagination, a singular, frightening idea began to crystallise into a complete obsession: he had to have that money.

The following morning, the two young apprentices had decided to close the shop so they could spend the day together in companionable leisure. They walked from Milk Street to the Black Swan pub in the Shambles, at the west end of Cheapside. There they drank a morning draught and made their plans for the day ahead. Noting that the weather was particularly fine, they at last decided to spend some time fishing in the River Thames. After they left the pub John treated Nathaniel to a new fishing rod worth four or five shillings. This was no small gift, for the cost of that rod amounted to approximately a week's wages for a skilled tradesman. Once the fishing gear had been purchased, they briefly parted ways to take care of some business, and met again at Paul's Wharf at around two o'clock in the afternoon. They popped into the Sun alehouse to buy bread to make groundbait before settling down at the river's edge to relax and fish. They delighted in the lazy warmth of an August afternoon, and watched the busy wherrymen as they taxied passengers to and fro across the river. On the south bank opposite their fishing spot they could see London's idle rich promenading or playing bowls, and hear the roar of men and beasts rising from the circular arenas of the ornamental bear garden. All that afternoon, as they sat side by side gazing out over the sparkling water, Nathaniel planned to murder John.

By six o'clock that evening they finished fishing and packed up their gear before heading their separate ways. A few hours later, at around eight o'clock, they met again at Honey Lane and from there walked the short distance to Fish Street, where they planned to have supper and drinks at the Maiden Head tavern. They dined on fillets of salmon and between them drank three pints of sack, a type of fortified wine that was exceedingly popular at the time. The famous diarist Samuel Pepys described sack as being more akin to hard spirits, and Shakespeare's Falstaff famously praised it as a drink to warm the blood, bring courage to the heart and ready a man for action. Perhaps Nathaniel hoped to gain a little Dutch courage for himself as he imbibed this expensive and strong drink by the pint. At ten o'clock they had eaten and drunk their fill, and so they staggered out of the Maiden Head and wound their way down Carter Lane to lock up Mr Goodday's shop, which Nathaniel was supposed to be in charge of. Afterwards they crossed over Cheapside and onwards to Milk Street to conduct their nightly ritual. Once the shop was securely locked, they made their way by candlelight upstairs and into John's small bedroom. There they stripped down to their undershirts, settled into bed and bid each other a good night.

As John slept soundly, Nathaniel lay awake. Hour after hour he sat with a pocketknife gripped tightly in his hand, and stared at John with a ferocious intensity. Several times Nathaniel lunged forwards with the knife, intent on thrusting the blade into his friend, yet each time his nerve failed him and he shrank back in horror. 'I made poffer many a time with my knife,' he later confessed, 'to the intent to cut John's throat.' Leaping out of bed, he paced back and forth in the room, and swore in his heart that he did not have the nerve to see the deed through. Sometimes he set the knife down, only to snatch it back up again in his trembling hands. This agony of indecision lasted until three or four o'clock in the morning, when at last Nathaniel struck. He plunged the knife into John's face and slashed his cheek wide open from his mouth all the way to his ear. With an agonised cry John was wrenched into consciousness, and to his amazement found himself locked in a deathly struggle with his dearest friend. Nathaniel had failed to deliver a killing blow, and he feared that John's screams might wake the maidservants sleeping on the floor above. Desperate to smother both his cries and his life, Nathaniel cruelly forced his hand inside John's wounded mouth and bore down with all his might.

The profusion of blood that spilled from John's slashed face mingled with the sweat wrung from his heaving body, making it extremely difficult for Nathaniel to hold fast; yet hold fast he did. During the struggle John fought violently, clawing at Nathaniel's face, neck and arms and tearing handfuls of hair from his head. It was an ordeal played out in frenzied silence: breath gasped through a smothering fist, internal moans of fury and limbs mutely thumping upon the blood-soaked mattress. It took Nathaniel almost half an hour of straining force to press the life out of his friend. At last the deed was done, and in a moment of delirious anger Nathaniel one again snatched up his pocketknife and sawed it through John's throat, working the blade upwards into the underside of his jaw and through his mouth to sever his tongue. This, Nathaniel said, he did for no other reason than to please the devil. Leaping from the bed, Nathaniel stripped off his undershirt and used it to scrub the worst of the blood from his naked body. He then got dressed and swiftly searched through John's folded clothes, where he found and pocketed the shop's keys. Silently he crept downstairs and unlocked the till, from which he withdrew two bags of money containing 110 pounds. Perceiving that he was drenched in too much blood, he discarded his gory shirt on the shop's counter before disappearing into the night as a thief, a murderer and a fugitive.

Thursday morning dawned, and the yawning maids sequestered in the attic of Mr Worth's shop set about their early duties: fetching water, preparing food and generally tending to the house and shop before it opened to the public. It wasn't long before the incongruous presence of the shirt on the shop's counter-top elicited confusion and then alarm. The maids raced up to John's room to report their discovery, and there they found his gory remains. They were staggered by the violent tableau of young John lying twisted, slashed and abused in a tangle of sheets, and gazed in wonder at the sheer volume of thick-set blood that polluted his bed. Their amazement broke, and the frantic hue and cry of murder was broadcast into the street.

At once a mass of curious spectators flocked to the silk shop and crowded into the doorway to see what was amiss. The discovery of bloody murder in the heart of London's wealthy mercantile district was explosive, and a frisson of fear shivered through the crowd. 'The murderer unknown, and escaped!' they cried, and any one of them could have been the victim. With that sobering thought came another horrific realisation: that any one of them could be next.

Once the initial confusion of discovery was past, the citizens of Cheapside looked to their public officials to manage the crisis. The coroner, Mr Edward Moreton, was called for and he quickly summoned and swore in a jury of twenty-four men from the neighbouring parishes. At this time the coroner's duties were not limited to simply holding an inquest to rule upon the cause of death. He also worked alongside other city officials and law-men to carry out a wider criminal investigation to seek John's murderer and bring them to justice. His investigation began with an examination of the body and crime scene. The coroner and his sizeable jury crammed into John's modest bedroom to conduct their 'first view' of the corpse. They observed that during his death struggle John's body had been twisted to lie with his feet upon his bolster and his head at the lower end of the bed. His body, undershirt and bedsheets were utterly saturated with blood. At first the coroner and his jurymen believed the deep cut in John's throat was the cause of death, and they assumed that he had quickly succumbed to that wound. This, however, was not the case. John's strangulation had been desperately protracted, and during the struggle he had fought violently to defend himself. He was not able to save his own life, but through his resistance he was able to provide the coroner with a vital clue: clutched in John's right hand was a lock of hair torn from the head of his murderer.

On Friday John's body was carried from the silk shop and laid to rest at the church of St Mary Magdalen. A multitude of friends, relations, neighbours and well-wishers accompanied this sad procession to the graveyard. Sighs and tears were mixed with a restlessness born of unease, for the murderer was still on the loose and the coroner's inquest, now into its second day, had yet to identify a suspect. Fearful rumours spread, and some believed that the killer was among the mourners who attended John's funeral. Emotions within the community were running hot, and neighbours looked upon each other with suspicious eyes.

In the days immediately following the murder, Mr Worth, at last, returned to London. He reeled with shock when he was told that his young apprentice has been brutally slain, but then he quickly recovered his wits and bent the whole of his will to the task of finding John's killer. He turned his shop over to the sheriff and the coroner so that it could be used as headquarters for the murder investigation. Mr Worth's shop had become the locus of action: here the inquest sat and deliberated the facts of the case, witnesses and informants were examined, the sheriff and his constables convened and citizen detectives gathered to orchestrate their manhunt for the killer. An ever-eager crowd milled about the open doorway in the hope of lending assistance to the investigation, to relay the latest updates to the concerned citizens of Cheapside and steer potential witnesses in to speak with Mr Worth.

A break came at last when a witness went to Mr Worth's headquarters to report that he had seen John last Wednesday, fishing at Paul's Wharf with another man. Mr Worth, along with the coroner and the sheriff, were keen to wring as much information as they could out of this informant. Did he know this other man? Had he seen him with John before? What did he look like? How was he dressed? As the witness described the man he had seen, all eyes fell upon a curious figure peering into the doorway; from top to toe he was an exact match of the description given by the witness. With a triumphant cry, the assembled crowd of citizen detectives fell upon this hapless onlooker and subjected him to the full force of their suspicions. However, it soon became clear that this bystander was not the mysterious man sited at Paul's Wharf; he was merely some poor sap who happened to bear his resemblance. With muttered apologies and embarrassed coughs, the shamefaced mob released their prisoner and sent him on his way.

In spite of this mishap, the information given by the witness was good. The mysterious man seen last Wednesday at Paul's Wharf may be a key witness, or, more tantalising still, a suspect. This new intelligence began to percolate through Cheapside, and by degrees the locals stirred themselves to recollect if they knew of a man who fitted the description. Upon hearing the latest news, a neighbouring servant came forward to tell Mr Worth that John was reportedly friends with a man named Nathaniel Butler. Perhaps, this servant supposed, Nathaniel was the mysterious man sighted on the fishing dock. After some further enquiries it was quickly established that Nathaniel was apprenticed to Mr Goodday on Carter Lane, and some men were quickly dispatched to fetch him. Nathaniel was not at Mr Goodday's shop, but could possibly be found somewhere close to Bread Street, where he had been sent to run some errands. The citizen detectives rushed across Cheapside and down past the infamous Mermaid tavern on to Bread Street. They scoured the street and charged in and out of shops and taverns searching for a man matching Nathaniel's description. Going inside a woodturner's shop, they suddenly came face to face with a man who exactly matched the mysterious stranger: there stood Nathaniel Butler.

Cornering their man, the citizen detectives breathlessly asked him 'Do you know John Knight?' At the mention of his friend's name Nathaniel blanched, and stammered a few words of denial before pushing his way out into the street. Undeterred, the citizen detectives followed and relentlessly questioned Nathaniel until he was forced to stop in his tracks and admit that he knew John. Pale-faced and shrinking with fear, Nathaniel insisted that he was far too busy and could not say another word on the matter. The citizen detectives were not to be moved and they stood firm to block Nathaniel's escape. There, in the muted light of the small alleyway, they looked him over with suspicious eyes and saw that his hands, arms and face were scored with scratches and cuts. In addition to these wounds, Nathaniel positively hummed with nervous energy, a combination that promoted him from person of interest to prime suspect. Yet the citizen detectives did not feel able or qualified to place him under arrest. They let him go and hurried at once back to Mr Worth's shop on Milk Street to make their report.

Upon hearing this latest intelligence Mr Worth called out to a few of the sheriff's men, who were at that moment loitering in the doorway to his shop, to instruct them to hurry to Carter Street and make their arrest. By that time, however, a spooked Nathaniel had gone to ground. He didn't emerge until Sunday evening, when he was at last spotted, seized and marched directly to Mr Worth's shop. He was stripped and every part of his body and clothes subjected to close examination. In addition to the cuts, scrapes and bruises on Nathaniel's skin, the coroner also found small traces of blood on his leather drawers and stockings. Mr Worth saw no benefit in a cautious approach: he stood boldly before a naked, shivering Nathaniel and accused him outright of the murder of John Knight. Nathaniel steadfastly denied the charge, but such protestations were made in vain as the evidence against him continued to accumulate. At the precise moment when Nathaniel was being examined by Mr Worth and the coroner, the city marshal had taken some men to Carter Lane to conduct a search of Nathaniel's room. There they found a trunk, which they swiftly broke open to reveal two bags of money, each bearing the mark of Mr Worth.

On his return to Mr Worth's shop the city marshal threw the bags of money on to the table and loudly proclaimed that they now had both the money and the murderer in hand. Nathaniel was tied with a rope, and while he was incapacitated a chunk of hair was pulled from his scalp so that the coroner could compare it with the sample taken from John's hand. It was a match. Confronted with this indisputable evidence, Nathaniel began to cry and in a most wretched fashion confessed his guilt to the coroner. After this he was marched in front of the Lord Mayor, Sir Robert

Tichborne, and once more compelled to repeat his confession. At nine or ten o'clock that evening Nathaniel was taken to the notorious Newgate Prison, where his legs were clapped in irons and he was locked into a stinking dungeon called the 'hole'. There he lay in darkness, staring with unseeing eyes and utterly stricken by how swiftly, and how catastrophically, his life had fallen apart.

Newgate Prison stood on the corner Newgate Street and Old Bailey Street, just a short walk from the Old Bailey courthouse. It was a truly frightening place, its name a byword for unimaginable suffering. Every class of criminal, from debtors to murderers, were crammed together inside its dark, imposing walls. There was no sanitation, no clean running water, no ventilation and almost no light. Inmates awaiting trial or serving out their sentences languished in vermin-infested dungeons, and 'goal fever' – typhus – spread like wildfire through the prison's malnourished population. One visitor to Newgate described it as a 'terrible, stinking, dark and dismal place, situated underground into which no daylight can come'. Everyday acts of violence stripped the men and women of Newgate of their humanity; they were oppressed not only by their jailers but by each other as well. Relief could only be purchased through the payment of exorbitant bribes; however, these small creature comforts could not inure the inmates to the brutality of their surroundings. In 1670 a newly admitted prisoner to Newgate described walking into the yard to see an executioner, fresh from the scaffold, preparing to boil quartered human remains in an enormous kettle. Before he plunged the severed heads into the water the executioner threw them to a crowd of felons, who laughed and jeered as they tossed the heads like balls, pulled their hair and beat them with their fists.

The 'hole' into which Nathaniel was chained was described in 1707 by a former inmate of Newgate as a 'dark, opace, wild room' that had to be climbed into through a hatch. The floor and walls were made from cold stone and a bare wooden pallet served as a bed, where the prisoner could sleep if they could stomach the 'stench that diffises its noisome particles of bad air from every corner'. Driven into the walls were iron rings, from which prisoners were weighted down with heavy chains. There was but one tiny window that did little to push back the oppressive darkness. A woodcut illustration depicting Nathaniel in the 'hole' shows a small man locked in chains, his diminutive figure overshadowed by a vast expanse of darkness which dominates the illustrative space. To be in Newgate was to be in darkness. One prisoner recalled that the blackness of the 'hole' was so overwhelming that he was seized with a 'panic dread' and was willing to pay almost any price for even just a little light. If he had been a wealthy man, perhaps he could have afforded the cost of a small candle; however, this sort of luxury was beyond the means of most prisoners in Newgate.

On Monday, 10 August the coroner and his jurymen reconvened at Mr Worth's shop to deliver the official verdict of their inquest. The verdict was no surprise: John Knight had been murdered by Nathaniel Butler. That same afternoon the Lord Mayor sent his personal chaplain, Randolph Yearwood, to visit Nathaniel in his dungeon at Newgate. Randolph's role was that of 'ordinary visitor' to Newgate, and his primary concern was to secure the confession and conversion of the condemned in order to validate court judgments and reaffirm the narrative that Satan's wicked influences had been utterly dismantled through God's divine justice. Thus the moral and spiritual conversion of condemned men and women was not a private affair, but a public performance that began in the prison cell and reached its dramatic finale at the gallows. Randolph cared for the spiritual well-being of his charges, but he was also a man on a mission who was determined to conduct a satisfactory and very public performance of conversion.

It was during his first meeting with Randolph that Nathaniel was made aware of the concept of forgiveness through grace. He could be saved, and his soul granted entry into heaven, if only he were to express genuine regret. This was a revelation for Nathaniel, who until then had considered his soul to be utterly lost, and from that moment onwards salvation became his sole obsession. He made a full confession, which Randolph recorded verbatim and later published for the edification of the general public.

In this confession Nathaniel described the day he and John went fishing and the violent murder that followed, in which he lamented: 'I destroyed the image of God in John Knight.' Here too he filled in the gaps of the story that hitherto had been unknown to the authorities. He said that after he had killed John he went home to Mr Goodday's shop on Carter Lane. There, in the courtyard, he washed himself and his clothes, taking special care to scrub the bloody stains on his stockings. He then went inside, removed all his clothes and climbed into bed with the bags of stolen money. The next morning he purchased a trunk, costing eight shillings, in which to hide the money. It was only then that Nathaniel became stunned by the reality of what he had done. 'I knew not what to do,' he wept to Randolph as he recalled that shocking moment, 'I came to Milk Street on Friday night, but knew not what to do.'

Nathaniel was arraigned for his life at the Old Bailey on Wednesday, 12 August. He stood upon two indictments: theft and murder. He pleaded guilty to both, and begged the court to favour him with some time so that he could seek spiritual repentance for his crimes, to which the Lord Mayor snapped back, 'You gave the young man no time of repentance.' It was a remark that struck Nathaniel to his heart, and he later recalled to Randolph that the Lord Mayor's comment had filled him with 'dread' and 'horror' as it occurred to him that John's unready soul had not been given the chance to be cleansed before death. This weighed heavily upon Nathaniel, who feared that this additional sin against John may have caused irrevocable damage to his own soul. On Friday, 14 August he was sentenced to be hanged by the neck until he was dead. Yet, in spite of the Lord Mayor's initial hostility, leniency was granted: Nathaniel was given just over two weeks' grace to put his conscience in order before his execution.

During the seventeen days leading up to his execution Nathaniel was visited many times by Randolph Yearwood and several other ministers. This was the time in which Randolph could coach Nathaniel into delivering a proper, and hopefully memorable, conversion. During these conferences Nathaniel was agitated into violent fits of emotional distress. He would beat his fists on his body in torments of self-pity before falling to his knees and meekly begging God for divine mercy. He was observed to suffer from heavy breathing and panting fits, on one occasion crying out, 'Oh! My heart will break. Is there hope for me? Is there salvation for me?' The devil, he feared, had been inside him his whole life and he was paralysed by the idea that, no matter how badly he wished for divine mercy, it could never be granted. He tried to take comfort in reading Scripture, and spent many hours kneeling in his dungeon while praying for absolution. During these final days Nathaniel was painfully torn between the dialectics of despair and hope – a state that was incited and heightened by his spiritual advisors.

It was at this time that the legend of Nathaniel underwent a drastic change in the public imagination. Nathaniel's spiritual advisors, led by Randolph Yearwood, spun a new narrative in which his emotional and physical torments in Newgate were reframed as beatific, cleansing events. Parallels were drawn with King David and Manasseh of Judah, biblical figures whose sins were cleansed through repentance and penal suffering. Biographical accounts of Nathaniel's life and crimes were closer in tone to hagiography or saints' lives than true crime. And, never missing an opportunity to drag Catholicism through the mud, Nathaniel's ministers cast their ward as a steadfast champion of the English Church as they recounted with enthusiasm stories of how Nathaniel repeatedly rejected appeals from his fellow inmates to convert to Romanism. Somewhere along the way, fear of and hatred for a murderer were transformed into pity and then admiration. Hands that were once slick with blood were newly imagined as gentled, meek and joined in prayer. The memory of John Knight faded into the background and was replaced with the story of Nathaniel Butler, the poor wretch whose sins were washed clean in the dungeons of Newgate.

On Sunday, 30 August, the day before his scheduled execution, Nathaniel attended his final sermon in Newgate's chapel. The chapel was by necessity divided by strongly built pens or cages, into which inmates were segregated by sex, status and degree of criminality. Attendance was mandatory, and those intent on sincere spiritual reflection were jostled by a reluctant and sometimes actively hostile congregation. The chapel was on the top floor of Newgate, and overlooked the yard from which those fated for death were loaded into carts or tied to hurdles – a sight that was incentive enough for many to keep their eyes turned upwards. Nathaniel did not glance out of the window and steadfastly ignored the press of the inmates around him, who boldly stood in his face and stared at him. Perhaps his fellow prisoners sought to intimidate him, or perhaps they wanted to see what moved behind the eyes of a condemned man.

That night, his last on earth, Nathaniel slept little and prayed a great deal. The Lord Mayor and Randolph spent most of the night at his side, bolstering his courage and offering words of comfort. While it was common practice for a minister to sit with a condemned prisoner through the night, the Lord Mayor himself would not have bothered unless the criminal in question was especially notorious.

Nathaniel seemed calm, stating that he was not afraid of death and was comforted by thoughts of the glories of heaven soon to come. As a gesture of repentance he wrote a letter to John's mother, submissively apologising that the 'hand which hath so barbarously murdered the son, should dare to write a letter to his mother'. In this letter he welcomed her anger, begged forgiveness and hoped that his current misery would bring her comfort. At five o'clock in the morning on Monday, 31 August the time of Nathaniel's execution had finally arrived. As his jailers closed in on him he succumbed to a final crisis of faith; giving vent to a high-pitched cry he begged, 'Oh sirs! Help me! Show me how to do it. I cannot do it enough. I cannot contain myself.' At the very last he doubted his own heart, and despaired that his lapse in faith might yet condemn his soul to hell. How could he believe in forgiveness by a higher power if he was unable to forgive himself?

At six o'clock the heavy shackles were knocked off his ankles and he was led out of the hole and into the yard. Within the hour a coach pulled by two horses arrived; a common murderer, Nathaniel was being afforded the unusual dignity of being driven instead of dragged to the gallows. The last of his restraints were unlocked and he climbed inside the coach, closely followed by Randolph, who according to his duty accompanied him on this final journey. From Newgate the coach moved through the crowded streets to Cheapside, where in that wide open space thousands had gathered to watch the final procession of the murderer of Milk Street. The gibbet where Nathaniel was to hang had been erected at the entrance of Milk Street, in view of both Mr Worth's silk shop and the church of St Mary Magdalen, where young John Knight was laid to rest.

The number of people who turned out to public executions such as Nathaniel's was truly staggering. Samuel Pepys wrote that he attended a hanging where he estimated there to be somewhere between 12,000 and 14,000 spectators. Viewing stands would have been erected further back from the execution site, where one could pay a fee to gain a better view. Those lucky enough to own houses overlooking the gallows could rent their rooms to wealthy citizens who desired not only a privileged situation but comfort as well. The wait for executions could be long and tedious; Pepys recalled attending another hanging where he paid a shilling to stand painfully upon a cartwheel and had to wait over an hour for the condemned to make their appearance. The atmosphere in the heaving crowds gathered on either side of Nathaniel's carriage would have been an electric mix of bloodthirsty hostility, impatience, excitement and pity. Randolph wrote that he saw many sympathetic looks on the faces that peered intently inside the coach; however, Nathaniel ignored them all.

Arriving at the gibbet, Nathaniel alighted from the coach

and into the noisome chaos of the vast crowd, who were held back by guards armed with halberds. The gibbet was a simple construction consisting of a temporary wooden structure in the shape of an inverted 'L' reinforced with a crossbar. A ladder was propped against the side of the gibbet, and standing at the top was the executioner, waiting with a rope ready in his hands. He was not a mysterious hooded figure all in black, but simply a city official respectfully conducting the duty of his office; wholly unremarkable and dressed in his usual attire. Looking up at his executioner, Nathaniel started to climb the ladder. Randolph moved to stand on the bottom rung, to keep Nathaniel from fleeing but also to keep the ladder steady and be available to offer comfort should it be needed. The executioner tied the rope round Nathaniel's neck and stood ready to hear the condemned man's final words. With a trembling hand, Nathaniel reached into his clothes and withdrew several sheets of paper before he turned to deliver his final speech to the thousands of spectators gathered before him.

The proposed speech was interminably long, nearly eight pages in total. 'Beloved friends,' he began, 'I am here a miserable creature . . .' and from there his voice was lost to the din of the roaring crowd. Nathaniel's hands shook, he sweated profusely, wiped his brow, fumbled his words and strained his voice, but no matter how loudly he projected himself he could not be heard. The multitude of people in attendance were becoming increasing restless and the noise swelled to unbearable levels as they pressed in on all sides. They had waited long enough and were impatient for the hanging to get under way. After a hasty and somewhat embarrassed consultation between Randolph and the sheriff, it was decided that the speech should be cut short. Randolph kindly suggested to Nathaniel that he should probably finish with a few words 'from his own brest, without book' ; something from the heart, and above all short. Nathaniel's composure was utterly shattered. He turned away from his speech and shouted his final words with all his might: 'Lord, if it be not too late . . . wash away this blood of my brother, which sticks so close to my soul . . . Let not the voice of my murdered brother's blood cry louder for vengeance then the blood of our crucified Jesus be heard to cry for pardon.' It was a speech that spoke of the depths of his fears, and even at the very end he hoped for absolution.

Nathaniel reached down and clasped Randolph by his hands in a final gesture of farewell. They prayed together, and after a few minutes Nathaniel murmured, 'Now I am launching into the ocean of eternity.' He straightened, lifted his arms and cried, 'Lord Jesus receive my soul!' The executioner then did his duty and turned Nathaniel off the ladder. He did not fall far, there was no long drop to break his neck, only a short length of rope that held him close to the gibbet so that he could asphyxiate to death in clear view of the crowd. If the executioner had done his job correctly, Nathaniel would have been unconscious in five to ten seconds, and dead within three to five minutes. It was not an instant death, but in the eyes of the law it was considered merciful when compared to the prolonged suffering that had been inflicted on John Knight. When at last death had come, the corpse was cut down, loaded into a coach and conveyed to St Gregory by St Paul's, where it was laid to rest. A final, fitting sermon was delivered by Randolph on the subject of hatred, murder and forgiveness.

For years after Nathaniel's execution his crimes were discussed, analysed and exhaustively picked apart in sermons, pamphlets, ballads and books. In the wake of John's murder pamphleteers invented fanciful stories in which John and Nathaniel were baptised in the same font, went to school together, played together and were devoted childhood friends. These were no more than fictions designed to add spice to an already dramatic story. Save for these few inventions, John's part in the story was quickly forgotten and all eyes turned to Nathaniel Butler, and there remained fixed. John Knight did not sell pamphlets, John Knight did not instil fear in the hearts of congregations, and John Knight's deeds were not terrible enough to bear the weight of a multitude of moral, religious and political agendas. All that could be taken as reasonably true about

John has been written here, but – constrained by the surviving record and the appetites of the early modern true-crime presses – that, shamefully, equates to very little.

This is a story centred on Nathaniel Butler and those who moved within his orbit. It is the story of the intrepid investigators who brought him to justice and his team of religious spin doctors who staged his final, redemptive act. Nathaniel was an unimaginably cruel and pathetic man who murdered his friend for the sake of money. He was by his own admission a drunkard, a gambler and a woman-iser who cheated and stole whenever the opportunity presented itself. His crimes were always in service to his appetites; when he cut open John's face and sawed through his throat and tongue he did so simply because he felt like it. It was a horrific crime that galvanised the citizens of Cheapside and city officials to work together to hunt down a murderer and thief. It was thanks to their collaborative efforts, clever detective work, forensic ingenuity and a little luck that John's murderer was caught and brought to justice. The details of Nathaniel's crimes are deeply upsetting, yet one cannot help but be moved by the accounts of his suffering in Newgate. His crisis of faith, his grief, remorse and violent fits of panic were likely genuine and deeply sympathetic. Yet Nathaniel's remorse was largely instigated by advisors who were keen to use a murderer's salvation to promote their own religious and legal agendas. Randolph's spiritual intervention seemed to have been heartfelt, yet his motives were not entirely altruistic.

In the wake of murder there was a process by which society could ease itself back into a rhythm of normality. The victim was laid to rest, the perpetrator punished, bloody hands and souls were washed clean, sermons preached, and in time a relative peace was restored to Cheapside. Yet there remained a few for whom reconciliation was a far harder process. John's mother and father had sent their son to London in the hope that he would flourish and perhaps one day return to them in prosperity and good health. Instead of welcoming a living son back into their arms they received a letter sent by his murderer. We shall never know if they gave their forgiveness.

POOR DESPISED
CREATURES

It was Midsummer's Day on 24 July 1609 when a young woman named Elizabeth Balleans stepped out of the cramped home that she shared with her father John, a stonemason, her mother Mary and her sister Francis. She walked alone through the ancient Norman parish of St Peter Mancroft in Norwich, one of the oldest and wealthiest in England's 'second city'. Following a great fire almost 100 years earlier, large parts of Norwich had been rebuilt and so the city contained a wealth of innovative new domestic and commercial proprieties that were built upon the surviving medieval foundations. In Norwich the rich and poor lived cheek by jowl. Grand brick and masonry buildings with jutting upper storeys, timber frames, tiled roofs and stone chimneys dominated the principal streets and flung their imposing shadows over the mean, subdivided properties that jostled for space in the back alleyways and rear yards of the city. It was from one of these poorer houses that young Elizabeth emerged. As she passed from the back streets on to the main thoroughfares of the city she could not have failed to notice the contrast between her own humble situation and the lavish wealth of the affluent classes surrounding her. Norwich was a rich and thriving city that owed a great deal of its prosperity to the worsted wool trade. In 1612 Sir John Harington described the city as 'another Utopia', invoking Thomas More's fictional vision of the ideal commonwealth. Norwich was by all accounts a fair and fine city, uniquely cosmopolitan and bustling with great markets and fairs.

The midsummer solstice marked the longest day of the year, signifying new beginnings and hope for a bountiful harvest to come. It was also a time of magic and superstition, of ghosts, faeries and misrule. Many towns and cities throughout England held to the old ways, and as Elizabeth hurried through the streets her senses would have been excited by an atmosphere of celebration and festivity. Doors were decorated with garlands of green birch, long fennel, orpin, white lily and St John's wort, and doorsteps cluttered with a colourful array of small oil lamps and trinkets. Some houses even displayed wonderful sculptures of wrought-iron trees from which hung hundreds of pretty lanterns. Bonfires, or 'bone fires', so named for the bones that traditionally fuelled them, were being readied. Once darkness fell they would be lit and kept burning throughout the night as watch fires to guard against evil spirits. Trestle tables and chairs were placed outside people's houses, ready to be laid with sumptuous foods and strong drink. Neighbours joined together to host parties and looked forward to a night of feasting and merrymaking. During the day grand pageants wound through the city. These were often spectacular affairs in which wonders such as model giants, snapping dragons and other fantastical creations were paraded with great fanfare past cheering crowds. In London one such pageant included an enormous serpent which spat fireballs from its yawning mouth. Musicians played and Morris Men danced to the accompaniment of ringing bells and clapping sticks. It was a time when friends and family came together to celebrate, to chase off mischievous spirits and to usher in good fortune for the remainder of the year ahead.

It seemed an auspicious time for Elizabeth. As the city revelled in the glad tidings of new beginnings she too was turning the page to a new chapter in her life. That morning she had bid farewell to her family and was making her way to the parish of St Michael at Plea, where she was to enter into the domestic service of Samuel Sandlin. She had outgrown the family home, and it was likely that her parents had been struggling to support her financially. Elizabeth was too old to live at home, yet too young to marry, and so service was the ideal solution. Employment in another household was a common stage in young women's lives;. a stopgap solution that ensured women were, at all times, placed under the control of a master. This was not mere social convention; it was forbidden in law for unmarried women to live alone and only widows were afforded some measure of freedom in their living arrangements. As Elizabeth walked the short distance to the home of her new master she must have been thrilled with nervous energy and hope that her position with Sandlin would be a happy one.

During her early days in the Sandlin household Elizabeth adjusted to the strangeness of her new position and duties. Service, she discovered, was a contrary life of ease and hardship. She was housed, fed and provided with necessary essentials such as soap, clean clothes, sturdy shoes and of course tea. She would have eaten well, sometimes even on meats and cheeses along with leftovers from her master's table. In truth, many servants were often better dressed and fed than when they lived with their parents, and they could save their wages to indulge themselves with the occasional small treat. In some ways it was a better standard of living, but it was also considerably harder. It is unknown what manner of household Sandlin kept, however at this time the majority of servants lived and worked in middling or small houses with a solitary 'maid of all work' taking on an exhausting range of duties. There was no clearly defined work day and Elizabeth would have toiled from sun-up to sun-down: cooking, waiting at table, caring for livestock, fetching water, cleaning the house spotless from top to bottom, doing the laundry, running messages, shopping in the market and weeding the garden, to name just a few of the duties she may have been expected to perform. At the end of the day she would have been exhausted, yet she would not have been permitted to go to bed before her master had retired. As her last duty of the day she would have been expected to warm his bed with a pan of coals and light the way to his room. Only then could she fall senseless into her own small truckle bed, to catch a few hours of sleep before rising early the next day to repeat the same cycle of drudgery.

Service offered many young women a better standard of living than they would have been accustomed to in their parents' household, however their position was also a perilous one fraught with danger. Maids had no separate accommodation in their masters' houses, no small space or bedroom to close the door upon and call their own. They bedded down wherever they could fit: in kitchens, hallways, cupboards and sometimes even in the master's bedroom. They existed in shared spaces where their masters had access to them at any time of the day and night. Young women in service were frequently viewed as no more than property, and were subjected to daily abuses, prying eyes and sexual exploitation. A London maidservant recounting her experiences in 1605 was told by her master, 'Thou art my servant, and I may do with thee as I please.' Another maid, named Dorothy Baker, was locked away at night so her master could 'have his pleasure of hir' whenever it suited him. The maidservant of one Leonard Whiting was so terrified by his frequent sexual assaults that whenever her mistress went away she would lock herself inside the milk-house. In 1651 a maid named Anne Barker was forced to sleep at the foot of her master's bed, where he used her 'constantly and familiarly every week'. When she fell pregnant he stamped his feet and raged at her 'be quiett, & content, & say nothinge, nor cry'. It was no great thing for these women to be abused and then cast off, for they were largely young, unskilled and uneducated: easily used and easily replaced.

Like so many young women in service, Elizabeth was isolated and vulnerable to abuse. She began her service at the end of June, and by the end of July Sandlin had forced his way into her bed and taken 'carnall knowledge of her body'. By the end of October Elizabeth was three months pregnant and beginning to show. As soon as the penny dropped Sandlin immediately terminated her contract and turned her out on to the street. He was quick to climb into her bed, and moved with equal rapidity to rid himself of her. She was not only an inconvenience, but potentially a source of great scandal; henceforth she was shamed as a 'bastard bearer', a 'harlot' and a 'whore'. Women such as Elizabeth were despised creatures who existed outside the accepted models of womanhood: not a maid, a married mother nor a widow. Her first steps into the home of Samuel Sandlin had been accompanied by the festive melodies of midsummer celebrations, but it was in the uneasy shadow of All Hallows' Eve that she found herself cast out, utterly alone and confronted by a terrifying new reality.

The fate of unmarried pregnant women in early modern England was grim indeed. Their bodies became objects of public suspicion and examination, to be grabbed, manipulated and squeezed by hostile hands bent on exposing their so-called shame. Many pregnant women, shunned by their friends and family, were forced to rely upon the charity of the local parish to save them from destitution. Such aid came at a high price. In 1609, the year that Elizabeth became pregnant, an amendment to statute law decreed that all mothers of bastard children supported by the parish were 'to be imprisoned in the house of correction for one year'. Other punishments for unmarried pregnant women and mothers included ritual acts of public humiliation and corporal punishment. They were dressed in white sheets and made to stand in church before the whole congregation, holding a candle or other sign proclaiming their sin. A case of ritualised penance from Middlesex tells the shocking story of Henry Wharton and Elizabeth Mason, whose crime of begetting a 'base born childe' saw them bound to a cart and stripped naked to the waist. They were dragged from the house in which the child was conceived through the streets and to the church, with their backs being cruelly whipped the whole way. In other parishes women were forced to walk in circles around the perimeter of the church while their backs and legs were flogged. By undergoing these acts of penance some women hoped to be symbolically washed clean of their sins, and in time perhaps welcomed back into the good graces of the community.

Those who would not be whipped or locked away found themselves in a truly desperate and lonely situation. Everywhere they turned doors were slammed in their faces. They were denied food and shelter, and were barred from supporting themselves through the few trades open to women such as victualling or brewing. The security of marriage was closed to them, for very few men would wish to saddle themselves with a 'bastard bearer'. Faced with no other option, many unfortunate women were forced into lives of vagabondage. Some managed to scrape a meagre existence selling odds and ends and others fell into the misery of prostitution as the only means to support themselves. To compound their suffering, a great many women had to endure the terrifying mysteries of pregnancy and childbirth entirely alone. In 1616 the parish clerk of St Botolph in Aldgate wrote of a poor maidservant named Rachel Snelhauke who was thrown out by her master, John Liddon. She had no female friends or relatives to rejoice in her pregnancy, no midwife to assist her in labour, and not even a roof over her head. She was delivered of her daughter all alone, out in the open against a church wall in the freezing cold of winter. This was a sad case, and the clerk later reflected that 'there are to manie of such servants now a days, more is the pittie'.

As Sandlin's door slammed closed upon her heels, Elizabeth, struck numb with fear and uncertainty, turned her face homewards. How would her mother and father react? Would she be cast out to fend for herself and her baby? Would she be imprisoned or whipped? Fortunately, Elizabeth happened to be one of the lucky few. Her mother Mary and sister Francis opened their door and, having heard Elizabeth's sorry tale, they drew her into their arms and deeper into their hearts. They knew what fate awaited Elizabeth once her pregnancy became common knowledge, and so they conspired to keep her condition secret, even from her father. As a stonemason John Balleans often worked away for months at a time on building sites or quarries, which afforded the women of his household precious time to adjust to their ongoing crisis and put a plan in place. A swollen belly and breasts could be hidden under stays and a voluminous dress, and could be further explained away as symptoms of wind, colic or dropsy. Elizabeth would have to keep herself hidden away as best she could, for the suspicions of her neighbours and friends might be easily roused. It was not unknown for unmarried women suspected of pregnancy or recent childbirth to be accosted in the street and their breasts squeezed by suspicious neighbours looking for signs of swelling or milk. Illegitimate pregnancies were considered a public issue, and women forced to hide their pregnancies lived in constant fear of exposure.

Mary was Elizabeth's saviour in more ways than one. She provided her daughter with shelter and safety from prying eyes, and as a mother she had the knowledge and experience to guide Elizabeth through pregnancy and labour. Many women in Elizabeth's situation were cut off from the wisdom of mothers and struggled through their pregnancies without fully understanding what was happening to them or why. Some women may not have been aware that they were pregnant, or they had disassociated themselves from their condition to such an extent that they were stunned by the unexpected delivery of a baby. One such example concerned a young woman named

Isabel Barton, who claimed that one day, as she was riding home from Scarborough market, she was pulled from her horse and raped. In the months that followed she saw that her body 'did grow big'; however she did not connect her rape with her changing condition and she had no idea that she was pregnant. When she suffered a miscarriage six months later the experience was wholly unexpected, frightening and confusing. In another case a Yorkshire servant girl named Grace Ward testified that 'she did not apprehend herself in labour, till the child fell from her as she was standing by her bedside'. These women may have downplayed the extent of their knowledge in a bid to distance themselves from the perceived guilt of their experiences, yet even so they were forced to endure their pregnancies and losses entirely alone, without midwife, mother or friend to offer them the comfort and support afforded to married pregnant women.

Elizabeth was able to keep her pregnancy secret for a further three months when, on Saturday, 18 January, she was walking in a yard in the pitch-darkness of night when she lost her footing, fell and landed heavily on a water pump, causing herself some small injury. At the time she thought no more of it and limped home to her mother and sister. Three days later, at around four o'clock in the morning, Elizabeth was curled up in bed with her sister Francis when she was struck with terrible pains. Her muffled agonies woke her sister, who cried out to their mother in the next room that Elizabeth wasn't well. Mary rushed to her daughter, asking 'What ails you?'

Elizabeth replied weakly that, 'All things were not well.'

Mary, frantic with worry, asked if she should call anybody to come help.

'Yes,' Elizabeth said, 'if you please, Mrs Richards the midwife.'

Mary and Francis quickly dressed and hurried to the house of Mrs Richards; however, to their dismay they found the midwife was not at home. Next they ran as fast as they could to the house of Martha Aitkins, another midwife who lived nearby. Mary knocked desperately upon Martha's door, and in time it was opened by her husband Peter. He was sorry to inform them that his wife had taken ill, and was fast asleep in her bed having 'taken something to swett' out her fever. 'She could not come', he said, before closing the door on them.

Mary and Francis were forced to go back home without a midwife, and within fifteen minutes of their return Elizabeth had delivered a stillborn male child. The three women sat together in silence, each contemplating the small lifeless body that lay between them. After half an hour Mary suddenly stood, gathered up the stillborn child and placed it carefully inside a box. She set this box aside in the same room in which Elizabeth and Francis slept, and there it remained for fourteen days while Elizabeth recovered her strength. Who can say what Elizabeth felt as she lay for so long in the dark of her room, her eyes lighting upon that small box and her mind circling around the fragile yet dangerous form that lay within. It wasn't unknown for mothers of miscarried or stillborn children to keep the body close to them since they were unable to move towards acts of burial or disposal. This paralysis held reality in check, delaying both acceptance and potential discovery. Elizabeth was not wholly unfeeling, and as soon as she recovered in body and mind she rose from her sickbed and took the box in hand. Those tiny remains were the only thing that stood between her and complete ruination. If she hoped to save her own skin then she would have cast her child's remains into the fire, buried it in a garden or thrown it by night into the River Wensum. Yet she did none of these things. Driven by her conscience and her courageous nature, she clutched the box to her frantic breast and strode out of the house and into the perilous light of day.

Elizabeth carried the body of her child into the neighbouring parish of St John Maddermarket. There she went to the house of John King, the parish clerk, and asked to speak to his wife Margaret. Once Margaret appeared on her doorstep Elizabeth opened the box and revealed the child inside. She begged Margaret to help her to bury her baby in the churchyard, believing that to inter the body in consecrated ground would set his soul free. Clearly Elizabeth did not consider her stillborn child to be no more than a 'lump' or a 'piece of gristle', as many at that time did, but rather she saw him as a being worthy of a proper Christian burial. We cannot know if she gave her child a name, or what degree of motherly affection she felt towards it, however her actions spoke of a woman determined to engage in the ritual processes of burial and grief. Margaret received Elizabeth's plea for aid with suspicious incredulity, and she immediately assumed the role of an interrogator: who was the father? Who was present when the child was born? And did Elizabeth (that fool) not think to summon a midwife? Why, Margaret asked, did it take so long for Elizabeth to come forward with the body? And why did she not approach the clerk of her own parish, choosing instead to sneak around neighbouring parishes like a thief? As Margaret stood on her doorstep and looked down at Elizabeth she did not see a grieving mother, but a suspected child killer soliciting an accomplice to help her dispose of the evidence of her crime. Margaret not only refused to help Elizabeth, she called the authorities and reported her. From that moment Elizabeth was exposed and taken to be questioned as a suspected child murderer.

Stillbirth and miscarriage were common occurrences in the early modern period, and while married women suffering these tragedies were not held to be criminally culpable, unmarried women immediately fell under the spotlight of suspicion. From the moment they conceived unmarried women existed in a liminal state of constant danger, straining under the threat of exposure, punishment and exile. Their status doomed them to exceptionally hard lives in which their own fates, and those of their newborn children, were uncertain. It was no wonder, then, that many chose to wrestle back control over their lives by resorting to desperate acts such as self-induced abortion and infanticide. When the body of a 'base-born' infant was discovered public outrage and suspicion swiftly followed, always aimed at its 'bastard-bearing' mother. Elizabeth was a young, unmarried woman who had hidden her pregnancy and concealed the body of her stillborn infant for two weeks. For a woman seen to have had every motive to want to kill her newborn child, her actions were viewed as deeply suspect. After her exposure two of the city's coroners were dispatched, and due to the unwed status of the mother they treated this case not as a natural death but as a suspected murder.

By 1609 infanticide was considered to be a crime equivalent to the murder of adults, and almost all unmarried women found to have given birth to a dead infant were accused of that crime. Yet there was a significant difference in how the crimes of homicide and infanticide were prosecuted. Those accused of homicide had several defences that they could put forward to demonstrate their innocence: they could argue that they had acted in self-defence, that the killing was accidental, or that they had not been of sound mind when they had delivered the killing blow. Women accused of infanticide, however, were denied such defences. A pregnant single woman was already deemed to be morally deficient and motivated to save herself from social exile by killing her child. Hidden pregnancies spoke of premeditation, and the concealment of an infant's body was sometimes assumed to have been proof of a guilty conscience. Infanticide was by its nature a secret crime and often the only witnesses were the perpetrator and the victim. Thus it was often unnecessary for there to be any other witnesses for the authorities to prove that infanticide had been committed, as the circumstances of a single woman delivered of a dead infant was deemed evidence enough to bring a charge of murder. How were innocent women who had suffered miscarriage or stillbirth to guard themselves from accusations that required almost no evidence to prove? And what of those women whose newborn children had succumbed to natural or accidental deaths after birth? It seemed they had no defence to save themselves from the hangman's noose.

Distinctions between premeditated murder and accidental manslaughter existed in law, yet they were rarely considered in cases of suspected infanticide. In 1570 a spinster named Maud Godley was sentenced to death at the Horsham quarter sessions after she was found to have murdered her newborn baby by 'obstructing his breathing by placing her right hand over his mouth and so suffocating him'. The delivery of illegitimate babies was often done in dread secret, and mothers who were exhausted by their ordeal and terrified of discovery may have stifled their babies' cries with a hand or some nearby item of clothing. Maud's actions had likely not been premeditated murder, but rather an impulsive and unthinking act in which she frantically sought to conceal her child from immediate discovery. Yet her status as a 'bastard bearer' was deemed to be motive enough for murder, and the presence of a dead infant in her arms was the only evidence needed to condemn her to death.

Another distressing case from the Sussex inquest records relates to a spinster named Mar Joan Browne of Etchingham. In 1588 she was accused of murdering her newborn male infant by 'wounding, crushing and breaking his neck and jaw and one arm' before she 'threw him under the stairs . . . where she left him'. The coroner in this case concluded that the child died from its multiple injuries, and Mar Joan was sentenced to death at the East Grinstead assizes. No consideration had been given to Mar Joan's mental state during and immediately after labour.

Married women who had violently killed their newborn infants were usually deemed to have been acting under the strain of temporary madness, and so were to be pitied and comforted. Unmarried women in the same circumstances were held to be no more than wicked, calculated criminals. The perceived difference between these women was moral: pregnant married women were mothers-to-be, pregnant unmarried women were harlots; one was inherently pure and the other corrupt.

Michael Beverley and Nicholas Morley, two coroners of the city of Norwich, convened their inquest into the death of Elizabeth Ballean's baby on 14 March 1609. They swore in a jury of twelve men from neighbouring parishes before beginning their investigation. The manner in which they conducted their inquest showed that they were cognisant of the crime of which Elizabeth stood accused, and they directed their enquiries with specific evidential proofs in mind. At this juncture Elizabeth was exceedingly vulnerable and bowed under the weight of public censure, religious condemnation and the threat of execution. Her reputation was utterly ruined, and her chances of surviving a murder trial were vanishingly small. Her situation as a single woman, her secret pregnancy and her concealment of the infant's body were more than enough evidence needed to send her to the gallows. It was extraordinary, then, that Beverley and Morley conducted their inquest in a sympathetic manner.

As per their duty they touched upon the proofs necessary to condemn her, but they also strove to include any small detail that might save her. Rather than seeking to destroy Elizabeth, Beverley and Morley seemed set upon discovering the truth, even if it ran contrary to the overwhelming culture of hostility that was aimed at unwed mothers.

In her examination Elizabeth confessed that Samuel Sandlin was the father of her illegitimate child. She swore that she had conceived at the end of July and that her labour was brought on in late January when she fell against the well pump. According to her timeline, Elizabeth would only have been five months pregnant when she was delivered of her stillborn child. A point of evidence that was commonly used to condemn women of child murder was to show that they had not prepared any clothes or essential items to care for their expected child. If an expectant mother had failed to procure any provisions, then it was assumed that she saw no need for them as she had already planned to murder her baby. In Elizabeth's case she had not accumulated any provisions, not because she intended murder but because she was only in her second trimester and assumed that she had plenty of time left before she was to give birth.

That that her baby had been born prematurely and was unlikely to have survived would not have been enough to save Elizabeth from a murder charge. Failure to take steps to preserve life, even a life so precariously fragile, was considered to have been tantamount to murder by inaction. Simply by delivering her baby alone and allowing nature to follow its tragic yet all too often inevitable course, Elizabeth was in very real danger of being hanged for murder. However, luckily for Elizabeth, the coroners Beverley and Morley took the time to seek out and include testimonies to prove that she did her best to save the life of her child. Both her mother and sister were questioned, and they swore upon oath that Elizabeth had sent them to fetch a midwife the moment she suspected something was wrong with her baby. The coroners then set out to collect the testimony of the midwife Martha Atkins. Martha confirmed Mary and Francis's testimonies and said that she had been summoned to attend Elizabeth; however, she was incapacitated due to her illness. Her word carried real weight, and her expertise in the sphere of pregnancy and childbirth was unquestionably valuable. These testimonies showed that although Elizabeth had hidden her pregnancy, she nonetheless had done her best to preserve the life of her baby.

At this point the body of Elizabeth's stillborn child was in the custody of Beverley and Morley. In cases of suspected murder the coroners would have examined the infant themselves; however such an examination was not recorded in the inquest record. They had instead yielded to Martha's superior knowledge in this field by permitting her to conduct the first 'view' of the body. Midwives were respected authorities and were frequently called upon to act as expert witnesses at coroners' inquests and in courts of law. Martha did not go into a great deal of detail, but she confirmed that Elizabeth 'did not goe her full time' and that in her professional opinion the child was stillborn. Such testimony was extremely important in cases of suspected infanticide, for technically the crime could only have been committed upon the body of a living infant. In instances of miscarriage and stillbirth the testimony of a midwife may have been sufficient to save the mother from a murder charge; however, very few women giving birth in secret benefited from the services or testimonies of midwives. And what of those women who had delivered live babies which later died of natural causes? In cases where there were no other witnesses to the birth other than the accused, how did the law distinguish between natural death and murder?

During the early seventeenth century, forensic science was an emerging yet still largely undeveloped discipline. In suspected cases of infanticide coroners and their juries relied mainly upon circumstantial evidence and witness testimony to reach their verdict. Single women accused of bastardy were already despised social outcasts, and so it was not surprising that verdicts underpinned by no more than supposition and hearsay did not go well for the accused. Yet on the Continent, where both the medical and forensic sciences were far in advance of those being practised in England, curious minds were conducting experiments with just such a question in mind: could medical science differentiate between an infant that had been born dead and one that had been born alive before being killed? Such experiments gave rise to the hydrostatic test, also known as the 'lung flotation test'.

The origin of the test was believed to have been based upon Galen's observations of the lungs before and after birth. He noted that 'the nature of the flesh of the lung changes from being red and heavy and dense to being white and light and less dense'. The idea was simply thus: the lungs of an infant that had died before birth would be dark and heavy, whereas the lungs of an infant that had been born alive and so taken in air would be lighter in both colour and weight. To show this the lungs of an infant were suspended in water. If the lungs floated it was taken as proof that the baby had been born alive. The following conclusion was that its death had been occasioned by its 'bastard-bearing' mother. Of course the test was highly flawed and did not take into account the myriad of physiological outcomes that may occur during and after childbirth, nor the very real possibility of newborn babies succumbing to unexplained yet natural deaths soon after being born. The first instance of the test being used in a court of law was in Zeitz, Silesia in 1682 when a fifteen-year-old peasant girl was acquitted of the crime of infanticide after the lungs of her deceased infant were found to sink when they were submerged in water. Although references to the hydrostatic test are found in texts dating from 1507, it was highly unlikely that women such as Elizabeth could benefit from, or indeed be condemned to hang, on the outcome of such a test.

Having examined all available evidence, the inquest at last reached its verdict: the male child of Elizabeth Balleans had been 'born dead'. Elizabeth's life had been spared, but her reputation had been irrevocably destroyed and any relief that she may have felt was bitterly tainted by that knowledge. The inquest had torn away her protective shrouds of secrecy and aired her sins before the whole community. Beverley and Morley's actions far exceeded the level of care that was typically afforded to the investigation of suspicious deaths in Norwich during their time in office. Perhaps such scrutiny belied a greater professional interest in Elizabeth's case, reflecting the period's overall obsession with infanticide and the perceived moral crimes of single women. Elizabeth's child was dead, and she had to navigate the rest of her life with a millstone of shame tied round her neck. This was an increasingly dangerous time for women such as Elizabeth as public hostility towards 'bastard bearers' had reached a boiling point, and things were about to become far more heated and far more deadly.

Revulsion towards 'bastard bearers' and murdering mothers was hysterically manifested through street literature, drama, ballads and true-crime pamphlets. Splashed across the front pages of lurid true-crime narratives were inflammatory titles such as *'The Cruel Mother'* and *'No Natural Mother, but a Monster'*. The villains of these infanticidal horror stories were almost always 'bastard bearers', 'strumpets' and 'whores' – that is single mothers – who were depicted as no more than brute beasts devoid of human feeling. Even wolves and serpents, it was said, instinctively preserved the lives of their offspring. Public opinion held that women who killed their newborn babies defied natural law and that their crimes were utterly incomprehensible. It is not surprising that street literature ignored the victimhood of these women and dismissed the desperate circumstances that drove many to commit infanticide. They were instead depicted as willing servants of the devil and inhuman creatures that bathed in the blood of innocents without a hint of guilt or remorse. Above all they were perceived to be dangerous beings, cancers that had to be cut out and disposed of for the sake of the commonwealth.

Public outrage towards the perceived crimes of unwed mothers was a hot political issue of the day. Parliament debated the problem and in 1624 passed a new Act 'to prevent the destroying and murdering of bastard children'. It stated:

> That if any Woman . . . be delivered of any issue of the body, male or female, which being borne alive, should by the Lawes of this Realm be a bastard, and that she endeavour privatlie either by drowning or secrett burying thereof, or any other way, either by herselfe or the procuring of others, soe to conceale the death thereof, as that it may not come to light, whether it be borne alive or not, but be concealed, in every such Case the Mother soe offending shall suffer Death as in the Case of Murther.

Even if a woman had delivered an infant that was already dead, if she had taken steps to bury it in secret or conceal it, then by law she was a murderer. This law was aimed almost exclusively at single women, and it was a law in which suspected infanticides were legally presumed to be guilty before they were proved innocent. Under such legislation Elizabeth, a woman whose crime amounted to no more than suffering a stillbirth and then placing the remains of her child inside a box, would have been far more likely to have been found guilty of murder and sent to the gallows to hang. The 1624 Infanticide Act proclaimed to protect vulnerable infants, yet in practice it was frequently wielded as a tool to control and punish unmarried women.

The 1650 case of Anne Green of Steeple Barton in Oxfordshire is a shocking example of just how ruthlessly the new law was applied. Anne was the twenty-two-year-old servant of Thomas Read and was described as a strong and sturdy woman of middling stature. During her employment she became intimately involved with Jeffery Read, her master's seventeen-year-old grandson. One day Anne was engaged in the physically demanding work of turning malt when she overreached herself and 'found herself to be very ill'. She rushed to the toilet where, confused and in great pain, she hid in the hope that the episode would soon pass. Mary, one of her fellow servants, became increasingly worried and crept to the privy to see why Anne was taking so long. There she heard Anne's distress and 'many heavy groans'. Within a quarter of an hour Anne, 'full of pain', had delivered 'a child, about a span long, but abortive'. That she had suffered a miscarriage was without a doubt: she was no more than seventeen weeks pregnant, the foetus was unformed, its sex could not be distinguished and according to witnesses it seemed to be no more than a 'lump of flesh' rather than a duly formed infant. It was likely that Anne had no idea she was pregnant. Her fellow servants testified that she commonly had irregular periods and that she had been experiencing intermittent bleeding prior to her miscarriage, which she attributed to an imbalance in her humours and nothing more.

Exhausted and overwhelmed by her ordeal, Anne fearfully laid the foetus in a corner and covered it with dust and rubbish. She emerged from the toilet in a 'very sad and deplorable' condition and was immediately confronted by Mary, who demanded to know what had been the matter with her.

Anne sobbed that she was 'Utterly undone, undone, undone!'

'Why Anne!' Mary cried. 'I hope thou art not with child?'

'Alas, alas Mary that ever I was born,' Anne wept, 'to live and die in shame and scorn: I was, but now I am clear of it.'

'Why? What is become of it?' Mary asked.

'Look yonder.'

Anne pointed to the privy, where the small remains of a barely formed infant lay covered. By covering the remains of her miscarriage Anne had, in the eyes of the law, attempted to conceal a body. Within a quarter of an hour she had been taken up before a justice, where she confessed to her pregnancy but denied murder. She was sent to Castle Prison at Oxford and at the following assizes she was arraigned for her life, found guilty of murder and sentenced to be hanged on the Oxford gallows.

On 14 December 1650, Anne's sentence was carried out. As she arrived at the gallows her courage gave out and she fell to her knees, begging God for aid. She was forced to climb a ladder and was duly turned off it by the executioner. As she swung from the rope her cousins, desperate to spare her suffering, grabbed hold of her legs and, using their whole weight, sharply jerked her body in a vain effort to break her neck. Other relatives beat at her chest and did all in their power to end her life quickly. The under-sheriff was so disturbed by the scene that he intervened and pulled her family back, leaving Anne to asphyxiate under her own weight.

What justice did the 1624 Infanticide Act hope to achieve? Anne had miscarried at seventeen weeks and was clearly innocent of murdering her child. Multiple witnesses had testified that she did not know that she was pregnant, and furthermore a midwife had sworn that the infant had been born dead. Yet the law was clear, and by the simple act of covering the foetus in a small amount of rubbish Anne had concealed a dead child, and thus was held to have been legally guilty of child murder. It can be argued that the severity of the law served a preventative function, which pre-emptively saved the lives of many unwanted babies that otherwise would have been killed; yet the absolute, unyielding way in which the law was applied in this case was deeply unjust.

Remarkably, Anne's story did not end with her death. After she was cut down her body was delivered to a group of physicians who wished to use it as part of an anatomy lesson. As they gathered about her and prepared to make the first incision, she seemed to exhale and make a rattling noise deep within her chest. Believing it to be a natural settling of the body after death, the physicians beat upon her breast to expel any further air, and were horrified to discover that she was alive and breathing. They successfully revived her and she lived the rest of her life under the notorious celebrity of her near-death. Seemingly God had intervened, and only then did public opinion shift to consider her potential innocence. Very few women, if any, were afforded such a miraculous reprieve.

The urgency to punish 'lewd women' had put in motion a veritable witch-hunt. Both Anne and Elizabeth had committed the moral crime of becoming pregnant out of wedlock and losing their children to natural causes; however their respective fates had fallen on either side of a ruthless body of legislation. It did not occur to the authors of this legislation to question the need for such a law. Why was there a proliferation of unwanted bastard children, and what reasons did unwed mothers have for killing their newborn babies? Lawmakers ignored the causes and conditions that led to infanticide, and focused instead on punishing women for their perceived moral failings.

What became of Elizabeth after the inquest into the death of her child is unknown, however her prospects were bleak. Her mother and sister evidently cared for her, but the ultimate decision as to what to do with her rested in the hands of her father, a man from whom she had done all in her power to hide her pregnancy. It is highly possible that she was thrown out of the family home and left to fend for herself. With no home, no prospect of marriage and no way to support herself Elizabeth had few options available to her. She may have sought the mercy of the parish and undergone the horrors of penance, or she may have moved to London where she could attempt to scrape together a semblance of a new life. Elizabeth was an unremarkable young woman who was cruelly used by her master before being crushed under the boot heel of religious and public censure. Her perceived crimes were uniquely those of the female sex, and by stepping outside the prescribed boundaries of womanhood, even when it was against her will, she forfeited any expectations of safety. The punishment was exile: exile from the Church, from her family and from the community that once embraced her.

Samuel Sandlin, Elizabeth's former master and the well-spring of so much suffering, had washed his hands of the whole affair. Had the child lived he may have been ordered to provide for it, however with no child to worry about he was free from any social or legal obligations. He likely suffered no more than a dent to his reputation, and perhaps some measure of marital strife if he was married. In cases of bastardy men were held to account, but on the whole they were spared the onslaught of fury that was directed at women who had played their part in creating a life outside marriage. The fathers of bastard children were unlikely to be cast on to the streets, locked into bridewells, hounded from their parishes or forced into extremes of poverty. The Infanticide Act of 1624 was passed exclusively to prosecute and punish women and women only. Women were, after all, deemed to be a disorderly lot, overflowing with a lewd sort of unrestrained sexuality that had to be contained and controlled by the state.

Elizabeth's wish to have her child buried in a churchyard was almost certainly denied. It was not permitted for unbaptised infants to be interred in consecrated ground, and so he was most likely given to Martha the midwife to be buried in a quiet, out-of-the way place such as a garden or a field. These burial sites were outcast places where the bodies of unwanted babies could be laid to rest, but ultimately forgotten. In the eyes of the law the value of miscarried, stillborn and murdered infants was at once priceless and of no worth at all. They were protected by the full force of state legislature, only to be tucked away in hidden graves; unmarked, unnamed and forgotten in the wake of so much anger.

THE BUSINESS OF
SINDERCOME

It was a bitterly cold morning on Tuesday, 30 January 1649, when King Charles I stepped through a window and out on to the boards of the executioner's platform, which had been erected flush against the side of Banqueting House, Whitehall. Seven long years of a bloody civil war between royalists and Oliver Cromwell's parliamentarians had led to this moment. England was fatigued by conflict, and stunned by the ruling of the newly established High Court of Justice in which the king had been put on trial for treason and sentenced to death. Charles was by nature a shy man, yet he faced death with courage and quiet dignity. That morning he dressed in two shirts, fearing that his shivers from the icy cold air might be perceived as fear. The executioner's block was low, forcing Charles to lie prone upon sand-strewn boards. His hair was neatly secured in a white cap and his neck stretched cleanly across the block to receive the killing blow. The axe fell and Charles's head was severed in a single stroke. As the executioner displayed the head a great groan rose among the crowd in attendance. Some grieved the death of their one true anointed king, and others celebrated the demise of a tyrant. England was declared a republic, and in a few short years Cromwell had forcefully stepped into the resulting political vacuum to seize power as Lord Protector.

Cromwell was for many a great man and leader: he was a masterful military tactician, a ruthless politician and a famously devout radical Puritan. But to men such as Edward Sexby, a disaffected parliamentarian soldier and former ally of Cromwell, the Lord Protector was no better than a bloody dictator. Sexby sought to free the republic from the stranglehold of tyranny by orchestrating a plot to assassinate Cromwell. While the battle-hardened Cromwell dismissed such plots as 'little fiddling things', his astute spymaster John Thurloe was keenly aware of the manifold dangers that threatened the life of his master. Thurloe's ever-watchful eye was fixed upon the machinations of Cromwell's enemies, and he used his wide network of agents to hunt down and destroy those hostile to the protectorate. Sexby had to tread carefully and recruit as his confederates only those whom he could trust to be unwaveringly loyal to both himself and his cause. The man he chose to lead his assassination plot was an acquaintance of old, a former soldier and rabble-rouser named Miles Sindercome.

Miles, a Kentish man, was a former surgeon's apprentice and later a quartermaster in Colonel Reynolds's horse regiment. In the aftermath of the execution of Charles I, he had revealed himself to be a rebellious and malcontent man. In May 1649 he had led a failed mutiny against Reynolds's regiment and was forced to flee, and in 1654 he was a principal player in a plot to turn the English army in Scotland against Cromwell. To his friends he was fiercely loyal, and to his principles he was steadfast and true. When provoked his temper could be explosive, but he was also a circumspect and deeply cautious man. His emotions may have run high, however they did not overwhelm his capacity for reason. He was a man of modest means and station, living above a hat maker's shop near Tower Bridge. He had a close relationship with his mother, brother and sisters, and, while unmarried, he was courting a sweetheart. In his faith Miles was a 'soul sleeper', a Christian mortalist who believed that the soul died alongside the mortal flesh of the body, to be resurrected once more at the Last Judgement. Threats of hellfire or promises of heavenly bliss did not affect him, and perhaps this sense of spiritual immunity gave him a mental edge as he embarked on a mission to assassinate a man who was king in all but name.

Sexby supplied Miles with generous funds and free rein in his choice of co-conspirators. Miles settled upon just three men: John Cecil, a fellow ex-soldier whose experience with firearms would be invaluable; William Boyes, a mysterious man and a master of disguise who went 'by several names and several habits' – appearing one day as a poor ragged priest and the next as a well-to-do gentleman – and lastly John Toope, one of Cromwell's lifeguards who had privileged access to the Lord Protector's schedule. These four men met in safe houses around London, and sometimes the Ben Jonson's Head pub in the Strand, to meticulously plan Cromwell's demise. Sexby, having set his 'jackles in the forest amongst the lions', was filled with confidence that his agents would play their part. He bid them farewell and soon departed for Flanders, leaving Miles in sole charge of the mission. In hindsight Sexby would later come to view his trust in his four agents as being wildly misplaced. Under the direction of Miles the plot soon became a farce of bungled operations exacerbated by poor luck and even poorer nerves.

Miles's first attempt on Cromwell's life was to take place on 17 September 1656, at the opening of Parliament. He had rented several rooms in a house overlooking the east door of Westminster Abbey, and had purchased several 'guns, harqubusses and pistols charged with leaden bullets and irons slugs', which he had transported through the streets of London inside a viol case. The plan was to shoot Cromwell as he exited the abbey after the sermon had finished. Cecil was positioned in the upper-storey window of the house with his harquebus, a large flintlock rifle that had to be supported upon the window ledge. Meanwhile Miles and Boyes, armed to the teeth with a hidden arsenal of handguns, stalked in the courtyard close to the east door. They paced in breathless anticipation, and like Sexby's jackals they clung to the shadows, hoping against hope to avoid being noticed before they could strike. At last the sermon came to a close, and Cromwell stepped through the east door and into the sights of three armed assassins. Miles moved forwards, and in a moment the Lord Protector was directly passing him. It would have been nothing at all for Miles, a seasoned soldier, to have reached into his coat, withdrawn his pistol and fired a killing shot into Cromwell. Yet in a frantic moment of indecision Miles hesitated and the opportunity was lost. In seconds Cromwell was swallowed on each side by the masses of people exiting the abbey. As one the assassins lost their nerve, and as they withdrew they swore oaths not to fail a second time. Cromwell, meanwhile, had no idea how close he had come to death.

In time, the conspirators hatched another scheme. Instead of shooting Cromwell in the crowded city streets they planned to cut him down during one of his regular Saturday morning jaunts through Hyde Park. Toope, as one of Cromwell's lifeguards, knew in advance when his master was preparing to take the air there. Miles was determined that he should not only succeed in his plan to kill Cromwell, but that he should make good his escape as well. He may have been dedicated to his cause but he was by no means a diehard fanatic, nor was he ambivalent to the idea of capture, torture and death. To this end Miles spent a fortune on several magnificent 'getaway' horses, including a bay costing £80 and another equally fine black horse costing £75. This was an extravagant expenditure, equivalent to over £8,000 per horse in modern money. In preparation for both their ambush and their escape the assassins trained their mounts as if they were racehorses, even going so far as to wear light clothes to give themselves a greater advantage of speed. In further preparation for their escape the hinges and hooks of one of the gates in Hyde Park had been filed away 'almost asunder', to ensure it could not be used to impede their flight. Now the conspirators only had to wait for the perfect opportunity to kill their target.

With swords and guns hidden under their coats, Miles and Cecil had ridden out to Hyde Park on five or six separate occasions. They pretended to be gentlemen out taking their exercise, slowly patrolling the shady avenues as though they had not a care in the world. At all times they were watching and waiting for a chance to get close to the Lord Protector, to strike and run before his guards could register what had occurred. It was not easy, for Cromwell travelled to Hyde Park by coach and was accompanied at all times by men whose sole profession was to preserve the life of their master. One day, at last, it seemed that fate was willing to hand the assassins a perfect opportunity. As Cecil was riding in the park with all the pretence of a man at leisure, Cromwell happened to take notice of his very fine, and very expensive, black horse. Being an admirer of horse flesh, Cromwell walked straight up to Cecil to ask him 'whose horse was that he rode on'. At that precise moment Cecil had both the opportunity and the advantage. Cromwell stood below him, unguarded and distracted, and yet Cecil did not act. His nerve had utterly failed him, and, muttering a few words about the provenance of his horse, he lamely made his excuses and turned to leave. Cecil later explained to a somewhat incredulous Miles that his horse had had a cold that day, and so he had prudently postponed the assassination until the poor animal was feeling better.

By early January 1657, Miles and his conspirators had botched six different plots to kill Cromwell. Desperate times, it seemed, called for desperate measures, and on the 9th they put in place their most audacious scheme to date. Miles planned to burn down Whitehall Palace with a 'firework' while Cromwell was in residence. His primary objective was to incinerate the Lord Protector, but he would also settle for destroying his enemies' stronghold. Miles had commented to Cecil that Whitehall was 'so strong a place, with so many turnings and windings therein, that it was the fittest hole for a tyrant to live in it' and that 'if it were burned, there is never another place in England where he could hide'. The firework had been designed by a specialist recruited from overseas. It was fashioned out of tar, pitch and gunpowder and placed in a uniquely woven basket with two slow-burning fuses. Miles intended to place the firework in the palace chapel at five o'clock in the afternoon, calculating that the fuses would trigger a blazing inferno at approximately midnight. Yet at the final moment Toope betrayed his confederates by informing Cromwell of the plot. Perhaps Toope had lost his nerve, or perhaps his conscience would not allow him to endanger so many innocent lives. Forewarned and forearmed, Cromwell waited for Miles to break into his palace and allowed his would-be assassin to set light to the firework before his guards rushed in to extinguish the fuses.

The game was up; Miles had been caught in the act and was soon placed under arrest. He fought wildly, and was not subdued until he had been bloodied, beaten and part of his nose sliced off in the fray. Meanwhile Cecil and Toope had been snatched up by Cromwell's spymaster Thurloe and spirited away for interrogation. From here there was only one destination for traitors against the Commonwealth. Miles was forced into a boat and taken along the Thames to Traitors' Gate and onwards into the frightening subterranean darkness of the Tower of London. Once an illustrious palace, the Tower was then a notorious site of incarceration, torture and execution. Passing below the great arch of the watergate, Miles disembarked upon a well-worn flight of stone steps. There he followed in the footsteps of history's most famous traitors: Thomas More, Anne Boleyn, Thomas Cromwell and Queen Katherine Howard had all once climbed those cold, damp steps. From there Miles was dragged to the Bloody Tower and shut in a cell as a close prisoner under the watchful eye of the Lieutenant of the Tower, John Barkstead.

Barkstead was a zealous Puritan who had once enthusiastically led his soldiers to close down the horse races, bear-baiting and wrestling rings throughout London. He had also previously worked alongside Thurloe in intelligence and security. As Lieutenant of the Tower he was reportedly a terribly cruel man who in later years was hauled before a committee of grievances to answer for his mistreatment of prisoners. His enemies called him the 'bum-bailiff' of the Tower, and a 'grand pimp of tyranny'. This was the man in charge of Miles, and over the next three weeks he endeavoured to wring a confession out of his prisoner. But Miles could not be broken. When threatened he merely laughed, and bragged to his jailers of his martial prowess and how many men he had killed on the battlefield. When priests were brought in to soften him by way of spiritual counsel he swiftly showed them the door. He would not be forced to betray his master Sexby, nor would he give up his friends. As an assassin Miles had been plagued by a timidity of spirit, yet as a prisoner he at last had found his mettle.

As his trial for high treason drew near Miles remained defiant. He scoffed at the very idea that he would be found guilty by a court of law, and was full of bravado as he boasted that he knew the laws very well and 'doubted not to make a very good defence' for himself. The Treason Act of 1351 held that it was treasonous to encompass or imagine the death of the king or queen. By law the offence of high treason could only have been committed against a monarch. With no king and no queen, how could there be treason? Besieged by threats to the Commonwealth, the new regime scrambled to redefine the offence. Treason laws were exhaustively drafted and redrafted, but without the accent of the Lords these laws were designated by Parliament as mere ordinances and not Acts. By and large the offence of high treason had been become absurdly broad and convoluted, including not only threats against the Lord Protector's life but also acts of political dissent and military mismanagement. Many treason trails collapsed before verdicts could be reached, or were dropped entirely before they could begin. Amid all this legislative chaos Miles felt confident that he would walk away from his trial as a free man and a hero of the republic.

On 9 February 1657 Miles was tried for treason at the Upper Bench in Westminster Hall. The evidence provided against him had been given by his turncoat friends Cecil and Toope. Miles said nothing in his own defence, although it was noted that he 'carried himself very insolent at the bar', and when he spoke it was only to deny the charges made against him. At length the prosecution rested their case and the jury retired to reach their verdict. To his horror Miles was found guilty of high treason and handed the following grim sentence:

> The said Miles Sindercome . . . be sent from hence to the prison in the Tower of London, from whence he came, and from thence be drawn upon a hurdle through the streets of London to Tyburn; there to be hanged on the gallows till he be half dead, and then to be cut down, and his entrails and bowels taken out, and burnt in his own sight, and his body divided into four quarters, and to be disposed of as his Highness the Lord Protector shall think fit.

Throughout his trial Miles had confidently anticipated an acquittal, so he was woefully unprepared to process the reality of his sentence. As he was dragged from the courtroom his temper exploded in a fit of fury. One witness described him as being 'enraged and in a great passion'. Miles had been sentenced to one of the cruellest and most bloody punishments practised in English law: he was to be hanged, drawn and quartered. For us moderns the idea of such an execution is largely an abstract one, no more than a curious barbarity that belonged to a far-distant age. To Miles his sentence was terrifyingly present and real. He may well have witnessed several such executions in his lifetime and he knew exactly what lay in store for him. As he was forced back into his prison cell he had nothing to do but wait, and picture in his mind's eye the excruciating details of the ordeal to come.

It would begin at the Tower of London. Standing at the door of his cell, the condemned man would have the opportunity to bid his loved ones farewell, to rub the tears from the face of his sweetheart or to press some coins into his mother's hands. He would then be stripped to his shirt and bound to a hurdle made from wicker, which would be dragged through the heaving streets of London to Tyburn. It is believed that the route to Tyburn passed by Tower Hill, through Cheapside, Newgate, Snow Hill, High Holborn, St Giles and Oxford Street. In previous years the condemned would have been dragged on the ground, but such treatment could not guarantee that a living body arrived at the execution site, and so the hurdle was introduced. It was a kinder mode of transportation, but not by much. The body of the condemned would still be knocked and bruised, and was vulnerable to the abuses of the vast crowd that followed his grim procession. The number of spectators turning out to witness a traitor's execution could be immense; when the Duke of Northumberland was executed for treason in 1553 it was estimated that some 10,000 were in attendance. The swell and roar of so many people, some crying for blood and others overwrought by expressions of sympathy, must have been an otherworldly and terrifying sight to those tied upon the hurdle.

Once the condemned man arrived at the gallows he would be untied and hauled on to a raised platform. There the executioner would be waiting for him, accompanied by the sheriff and chaplain. A proclamation would be read out, and the surging crowd instructed to step back. The torture of the condemned would then begin. He would be compelled to climb a ladder and a noose would be placed about his neck, with the knot situated below his ear. He would then be afforded an opportunity to make a final speech. Most men used this time to voice penitent words, while those who spat invectives or uttered rebellion were forcible gagged. With such formalities out of the way the executioner would turn the prisoner off the ladder, leaving him to choke and strain until he was nearly dead. This part of the sentence was a tricky business, for the prisoner must be hanged but not killed. It would have been a complete disaster for the executioner to accidentality kill the condemned man too soon. When he judged the moment just right, the executioner would give a signal to the 'top man' seated upon the gallows to cut the prisoner down.

If the condemned man was unconscious, he would be revived before his disembowelling could begin. This butchery may have been done on the floor of the executioner's platform, or on a table that afforded the crowd a better view. A brazier burned hotly nearby, ready to receive the entrails and body parts cut from a still-conscious and feeling body. First the genitals would be sliced off, a symbolic act signifying the end of a traitorous line. Next the stomach would be slit open, and the bowels pulled out before the condemned man's eyes. During these horrific moments the inexperience of the executioner often served to compound the suffering. In the case of Richard White in 1584, his executioner, 'having made a little hole in his belly . . . pulled out of the same his bowels by piecemeal; the which device taking no success, he mangled his breast with a butcher's axe to the chine most pitifully'. In 1587 Thomas Prichard's executioner made such a botch of things that Prichard was forced to help him finish the job. Desperate to expedite his own death, Prichard reached into the cavity of his own bowels and with a wretched cry of *miserie mei* flung his guts on the floor. Those condemned to die by this method could only hope and pray that their own executioner was not so incompetent. The intestines would be thrown into the brazier alongside the genitals and whatever other parts had been cut away. There they would smoulder and smother those standing close by with the stench of broiling meat and shit. At last the heart, still 'leaping and panting', would be carved from the body and the head smitten off with an axe, both of which would be seized by the executioner and displayed to the crowd.

Next the headless corpse would be cut into quarters. There was no one definitive way of doing this, but several contemporary etchings depict the executioner using a heavy butcher's axe to split the body along the spine like a hog. Once the corpse had been cut in half down the middle it could easily be cut into quarters. These parts, along with the head, were loaded into a cart and driven to Newgate. There they were thrown into a large kettle pot to be parboiled with bay salt and cumin, a fragrant melange that preserved the flesh and helped to repel scavenging birds. The heads of traitors would be taken to Tower Bridge, where they were placed on spikes to serve as a dire warning to all who looked upon them. The quartered body parts would, by order of the monarch or Lord Protector, be displayed in locations that were specific to the dead man, such as where he lived or where he had plotted treason. There his arms and legs would be skewered to poles, hung from chains or locked within gibbets. Only when these gory parts had served their purpose would they be 'thrown down' into the street. There it was hoped that friends and family could at last reclaim the remains of their loved one and carry them away for a secret burial.

The imagined prospect of such an ordeal quickly doused the heat of Miles's outrage. His fury subsided and was replaced by a desperate need to escape from his wretched circumstances. He begged his keeper, Daniel Steer, to bring him some poison so 'that he might make away with himself'. Steer, seeing no reason why he should aid his prisoner, flatly refused. That same day Miles's sister, Elizabeth Herring, arrived at his cell to pay a visit. Looking at her pale and tear-stained face, Miles once again fell into a great passion. They clung to each other and whispered urgent confidences, swearing between themselves that he surely must not come to such a cruel and bloody end. Elizabeth cried that their mother would not be able to survive the death of her son, and that she and all their friends would be deeply shamed by it. Swallowing his pride, Miles asked his sister to fetch him poison; however, she was unable to force a reply through the grief clogging her throat. She shook her head and withdrew in stricken silence. Once outside the cell she rushed to Steer and wept .'Lord! What shall I do? Did you hear him, what he said of the poison?' Determined to nip any schemes of suicide in the bud, Steer warned Elizabeth that should Miles be found dead by his own hand, then she would be held responsible. Stung by Steer's threat and weighed down by a terrible burden of misery, Elizabeth fled from the Tower. Only she could save her brother from the horrors of his execution, but to do so she would have to hand him the means to destroy himself. Suicide was no small measure – indeed for the early moderns there could be no greater crime against man or God.

Suicide was a subject that generated a great deal of heated moral and religious debate, not to mention a near-pathological measure of fear and loathing. The force of public hatred against suicide could be found in sermons preached from the pulpit, in treatises and books, on the stage, in songs and ballads, and in popular true-crime pamphlets. One such publication urged its readers to read grim tales of suicide 'with a holy dread . . . horror and detestation'. Popular opinion in Tudor and Stuart England held that suicide was a wretched crime driven entirely by malice and a total rejection of Christian moral values. It supposedly destroyed communities and invited divine vengeance. In secular law suicide was a felony offence. The word suicide, from the Latin *suicidium* or 'the killing of oneself', was not in common use during the seventeenth century. It was instead called *felo de se*, meaning to 'commit a felony against oneself'. As well as in law, suicide or self-murder was also severely condemned by the Church, which perceived the act to be a spiritual offence against God. Because self-murder was so reviled by both Church and state, those who committed it were, in death, subjected to religious and secular punishments.

In retribution for their crimes, self-murderers were cast out of the Church in both body and soul. They were denied proper Christian burial, and their bodies were desecrated by profane burial practices that were designed to humiliate the dead and traumatise the living who bore witness. These rituals of profane burial were not written into law, but they were nonetheless popular customs sanctioned by Church and state. The bodies of suicides were dragged naked through the streets, to be mutilated and spat upon before they were tumbled into makeshift holes or buried at lonely crossroads. In some instances the bodies of the dead had iron-tipped stakes driven through them, pinning them to the earth of their shallow graves. The tip of the stake was left exposed above the grave as a marker of shame, and as a warning to others against taking their own lives. It was forbidden to bury a suicide on consecrated ground: they were excommunicates who were denied their place in the community of the Christian dead. The Church forbade prayers for suicides, as it cruelly insisted that no words of grace could ever touch those souls exiled to hell.

One such case of profane burial occurred in September

of 1590 in the parish of St Botolph without Aldgate in London. Amy Stokes, a sixty-year-old woman, had been found hanging from a beam in her private chambers above a 'saw pit', or timber yard. The coroner who examined her body did not consider her to have been a soul in crisis; rather he condemned her as a calculating criminal who in taking her own life had acted with forethought and malice. She was not a victim of circumstance or mental illness: she was a felon, a murderer and a sinner. His verdict stated that she had 'hanged and murthered herself', and so he issued a warrant sentencing her corpse to suffer profane burial:

> By the said crowner that she [Amy Stokes] should be carried from her sayd howse to some cross way neare the townes end and theare that should have a stake dreven thorowgh her brest and so be buried with the stake to be seene for a memoryall that others goinge by seeinge the same myght take heede for comittinge the lyke faite.

That same evening, at about six o'clock, Amy's body was manhandled through the streets to a crossroads near Sparrow Corner, close to the Tower of London. She had no coffin, nor even a winding sheet to shield her from the disdainful looks of those who had turned out to watch her undignified procession. As a hushed crowd looked on her body was tossed into a hole and the point of a huge iron-tipped stake balanced upon her breast. With one man holding the stake, another drove it through her chest and out through her back with the mighty blows of a large mallet. Once Amy had been covered in earth, the stake stood proud of her burial mound; a pitiful memorial, for it signified not a life to be mourned but a crime to be reviled.

Fear of desecration and excommunication did not weigh so heavily upon Miles's conscience. As a 'soul sleeper' he had no fear of suicide, for he had no fear of hell. What he did fear was the pain and humiliation of public execution, and above all else he desired the autonomy to end his life by the time and method of his choosing. But he was closely guarded at all times, and despite his best efforts he was unable to procure the poison he so badly needed. By the orders of Lieutenant Barkstead he was watched night and day by the ever-vigilant Steer. The order for Miles's execution could come at any moment, and without the method or opportunity to kill himself he grew increasingly desperate. Unable to take his own life, Miles instead set about planning a daring escape from the Tower.

In order to enact his plan he needed to bring Steer on to his side by way of a generous bribe. Miles was by no means a wealthy man, but he was flush with Sexby's money and felt no qualms about using it to pay off his keeper. Desiring a moment alone in his cell, Miles asked the guards on duty to withdraw a little to a nearby window. They evidently saw no danger in stepping away and obliged their prisoner this request. Once alone, Miles turned his back on them and hastily set about composing a secret letter. 'Mr Steer,' he wrote, 'you see my condition, it is no time to dally!' In this letter Miles promised Steer £200 upfront, with £500 more to follow if he were to arrange for a suit of black clothes, a periwig and a dagger to be hidden in the room below his own. Miles planned to pry loose the floorboards of his cell and slither down through the hole, dress in his disguise and then steal away from the Bloody Tower, down the steps to the Traitors' Gate and away into the night by boat. He said that once he had made his escape he would trouble Steer no more, but vowed he would kill any man who stood in his way. Sadly, Miles was unable to finish his letter; his guards by the window had grown suspicious and drew close by to see what occupied their prisoner's attention. Upon seeing the letter they grabbed hold of Miles and hauled him away, dragging his stylus from the page mid-sentence.

On Friday, 13 February 1657, Miles was at last given notice that his execution was to take place the following morning. It was usual practice for those sentenced to death not to be notified of the time of their execution until the very last moment – in some cases not until a few hours beforehand. This was done deliberately, for those hours between notification and death were a dangerous time. Men and women robbed of their last hope may be driven to commit desperate acts. Knowing that Miles was a deeply passionate man who had threatened suicide and escape, Barkstead instructed his guards to keep an especially close eye on him. Miles was a suicide risk and the Lieutenant of the Tower was nervous that he might, in his final hours, find some way to kill himself.

That night, at around eight o'clock, Miles was visited by his beloved sister Elizabeth and his sweetheart. They sat together, and with 'trouble and sorrow' lamented their wretched circumstances. Grasping her brother by his hands, Elizabeth leaned in to him and whispered that she 'had rather see him die before she went from him, than he should die so barbarous a death as was intended for him'. As she spoke these words she slipped into his hand a small packet of poison. Elizabeth knew full well that she would be held accountable, and by her actions she was exposing herself to terrible danger. Yet love had won through, and with her brave words she passed to her brother the means by which he could escape the agony of a traitor's death. Her fear must have been plainly written upon her face, for the guards perceived a strangeness in her expression and rushed to separate the two. She was searched, yet the exchange had already been made and the guards found nothing on her person. The visit was abruptly over, and without another word the women were escorted out of the room. As soon as the guards returned they conducted a thorough search of Miles, yet remarkably they did not discover the poison.

Soon afterwards Miles was observed kneeling by his bed as though in prayer. His brow was slick with sweat, his limbs trembled and jerked, and his gut retched with anxiety. Later, at about nine or ten o'clock, he asked his guards to withdraw from his cell as he wished for solitude to pray. They obliged him, and as they waited outside they received an urgent message from Lieutenant Barkstead warning them to guard their prisoner closely, for his earlier meeting with his sister has been noted and his behaviour was deeply suspicious. Barkstead strongly suspected that his prisoner would try to try kill himself with poison and was determined not to let this happen. Miles's life was not his own to take, for the state demanded a living body for the grand execution that was scheduled the following day.

After about fifteen minutes Miles called out to say that he was done with his prayers. When the guards entered the cell they saw Miles wildly pacing about, rubbing his hands together and wiping his nose and mouth with a handkerchief. He continued in this agitated state for another fifteen minutes before he abruptly grabbed his Bible and slumped into a chair. As he read he seemed to find some measure of peace, and after a short time he got to his feet and told his guards that he was ready to go bed.

Standing as though in a daze, he marvelled 'that this was the last night he should ever go to bed, and the last bed he should lie in'. He lay down, and by the sound of his snoring his guards believed that he had fallen asleep. Yet his snores quickly became violent snorts, and then a strained rattle deep in his throat. Alarmed, Steer grabbed a candle and hurried over to find Miles laying half dead upon his sheets. Steer quickly summoned a doctor; however it was too late. Miles lay in a paralysed silence for a further two hours before he died. In that time he had wrested victory from the hands of his enemies and claimed it as his own: his living body would remain untouched by the executioner, and his soul reposed in painless oblivion.

Barkstead was outraged and at once summoned a coroner for the City of London, Thomas Evans, to conduct an inquest into Miles's death. Although it was presumed that Miles had taken poison, the coroner's jury were none-theless duty-bound to examine all available evidence before reaching a verdict. Evans charged his jurymen to 'diligently attend' to the manner of death. To assist him in his inquest, Evans had summoned two of London's most eminent medical practitioners to conduct a post-mortem. They were the famed astrologer and medic Sir Richard Napier and Dr Christian Fern, who was Reader of Anatomy at Gresham College. Upon opening the body neither Napier nor Fern could find any evidence of poison; however, when they opened the skull and examined the brain they found it to be 'red, and distended with blood, swoln and full as the skull could well hold'. They stated that the condition of the brain exceeded that of ordinary diseases such as apoplexy, and concluded that it had been damaged by some violent and preternatural cause. They held that Miles must have caused damage to his own brain 'by some extraordinary means', most likely, but not conclusively, by snorting poison up his nose.

As the inquest drew into its second day it was decide that Miles's body should be transferred to a brighter and airier room. Several items of large furniture were moved to clear the way, and it was during this relocation that a suicide note was discovered hidden underneath a close-stool, a type of portable toilet in the shape of a chair. The note, apparently written and signed by Miles, read:

God knoweth my heart, I do take this course, because I would not have all the open shame of the world executed upon my body; I desire all good people not to judge amiss of me; for I do not fear my life, but do trust God with my soul. I did this thing without the privity of any person in the world: I do, before God and the world, clear my keeper, my sisters, my mother, or brother, or any other of my relations, but it was done alone by myself. I say by me, the 13th day, 1657. Miles Sindercome.

He knew that his loved ones, especially his dear Elizabeth, would be accused of assisting him in a felony offence. By his final letter he had hoped to absolve them of that charge. True to his word, Steer accused Elizabeth of smuggling poison to her brother; however, in spite of being subjected to interrogation she steadfastly denied any wrongdoing, and neither did Miles's other sisters or mother crack under examination. Without proof and without a confession the authorities were unable to prosecute Elizabeth for any crimes. She had risked much to spare her brother the indignity of execution, and thanks to her cool nerve she achieved her aim and walked away as a free woman. But success in this endeavour could scarcely be counted as a win. She did what she felt was best, yet it was by way of her own hand that her brother had committed suicide. She had to live out the rest of her days carrying that burden of responsibility.

For several more days the coroner and his jurymen deliberated on the evidence presented to the inquest. They viewed the suicide note, read the surgeon's reports and reviewed the examinations of Miles's guards and family members. No stone was left unturned, and on Tuesday, 17 February the jury unanimously agreed that Miles did 'feloniously snuff and draw' a poison to 'kill and murther' himself. They ruled that he was guilty of committing *felo de se*. By this decision Miles had been condemned once more; for he was not only a traitor to the Commonwealth, he was also guilty of committing that most hated and reviled of crimes: self-murder. Following this verdict the coroner issued a warrant to subject Miles's body to profane burial. The citizens of London had been denied the execution of a traitor, and so they turned out in their thousands to witness the sorry spectacle inflicted upon those found guilty of killing themselves.

Miles's body was hauled from the Tower and out on to the street, where the raw scars of his post-mortem were exposed for all to see. He was not tied to a wicker hurdle as there was no longer any need to preserve his flesh; he was simply roped to the back of a horse, and as he was dragged along the filthy streets his body was cruelly bashed and torn. This parade of ritual desecration was no longer directed to Tyburn, but instead followed the much shorter route to Tower Hill. There a scaffold had been erected, much the same as the one at Tyburn where he was meant to have been hanged, drawn and quartered. Beneath the scaffold a hole had been dug. Without a word of Christian prayer his corpse was 'turned in' to the hole 'stark naked' and left to lie in an undignified heap. Next, a huge stake 'spiked with iron' was driven through his body and down into the freezing earth. As the gravedigger started to fill in the hole he left part of the stake exposed above ground, so that it 'may stand as a example of terror to all traytors for the time to come'.

This macabre ritual had been performed in much the

same way as many other profane burials throughout England. Yet it is striking that aspects of this desecration also mirrored the execution that Miles was supposed to have endured. The state, in its zeal to inflict punishment upon both a traitor and a self-murderer, had neatly overlaid the theatre of execution with the solemnity of profane burial. Robbed of a living body upon which to inflict their wrath, they had to make do with a dead one. It must have been a strange and sobering event to witness, and yet lacking in so many ways. The masses had gathered in their thousands to experience the thrilling catharsis of torture, death and butchery and instead had to watch the cold interment of an unfeeling corpse. Of course Miles had hoped to live, and given the choice he would have seized the chance to escape, perhaps even returning to the side of his master Sexby in Flanders to plot even more daring schemes. Yet in his final days he vowed that he did not fear death, only pain and humiliation. By killing himself he had struck a blow against his enemy Cromwell, and unbeknown to him fired the political zeal of others who envisioned the death of the Lord Protector. By taking his own life Miles gave courage to his friends and comfort to his loved ones, who at the very least were spared the horrors of seeing his life's blood splashed upon the executioner's platform.

THE TRIAL OF
SPENCER COWPER

It was a subdued and damp morning on Tuesday, 14 March 1699 as dawn broke over the small yet prosperous market town of Hertford. As the muted sun climbed the horizon, the tradesmen and women of the town rolled out of their beds, snatched a small breakfast and set their hands to the labours of a new day. Malting and brewing were the heart and soul of Hertford and a great many businesses and private homes were occupied in the beer trade, which owed much of its wealth to Hertford's surrounding fields of high-quality barley. The town's rooftops were dotted with the distinctive cone-shaped kiln flues of malting houses, from which white plumes of steam and smoke surged into the sky and infused the streets below with the earthy, sweet aromas of boiling wort and hops. Hertford's proximity to major land trade routes ensured a steady flow of travellers to the town, who could rest their weary feet, and of course taste the local brew, at one of the twenty-five inns, alehouses and staging posts that jostled for trade along Fore Street. Heavy barge traffic crowded on to the River Lea, which ran through the centre of the town and onwards to the River Thames and London. Malt barges navigated the river's narrow confines and shallow depths; traffic jams and flared tempers were a common sight. The flowing river not only served as a major transport route; it was also channelled via millponds and sluice gates to power the many watermills in operation alongside its banks. The beer trade was big business, and the whole of Hertford thrummed with the sights, sounds and smells of brewing.

The weather the day before had been exceptionally wet and gloomy, and as a result the River Lea ran higher and with more force than usual. James Berry, the owner of the Priory watermill on Folly Island, had risen early and was out of the door by six o'clock to 'shoot a flush', clearing the river of the build-up of detritus washed downriver after the rain. As he stood on the bank he ran his professional eye over the water, and saw in the dim light of morning a near-ethereal gathering of fabric. It seemed a bundle of cloth was caught up against a row of evenly spaced stakes nailed to the underside of a nearby bridge that served to trap 'weeds and trumpery' from entering the millpond beyond and damaging the mill. As Berry drew closer to the bridge, he was amazed to discover that the bundle was in fact the petticoats of a young woman dead in the water. Stunned by his discovery, Berry cried out in alarm to some nearby workers. A crowd of about twenty people quickly gathered, eager and frightened to discover the identity of the unfortunate soul. Several men convened on the bridge and, reaching down, they were able to untangle the body from the stakes and haul it out of the water. The woman was covered in such a quantity of river slime that none in the crowd could at first guess her identity. She was dressed in a striped petticoat and apron, and her stockings were partway rolled down. It was clear from the quality of her clothes that she was a well-to-do lady, but who was she? As the onlookers gently cleaned her face they were soon electrified by the shock of recognition. The woman was their neighbour and a well-known member of Hertford society. Her name was Sarah Stout.

In life Sarah had been a beautiful, fashionable and popular young woman who enjoyed entertaining friends and conducting business at her home in Hertford and in London. She was just a few days shy of her twenty-sixth birthday when she died. She lived in a respectable house about a quarter of a mile outside the centre of Hertford with her mother, father and live-in servants. Her father was a wealthy maltster, and while Sarah enjoyed the comforts afforded to her by her father's fortune, she nonetheless had to live under the rule of his paternal authority. Sarah belonged to a prominent Quaker family, and like many young people growing up in minority sects she chafed against a religion that held her apart from the majority of her peers. Within her faith she was afforded a greater measure of spiritual equality, but as a young woman interested in friendships and romance she often felt the chill of social isolation. This was further compounded by her father's heavy involvement in Whig politics, a position that frequently set him and his family in opposition to the ruling Tory elite of Hertford. By birth and not by choice Sarah was a Nonconformist and a political outsider. She conducted herself dutifully, but in private she often vented to her non-Quaker friends of a growing frustration with her station in life.

Sarah's body was carried to a nearby barn, where she was laid out and stripped in preparation for the coroner, who had already been sent for. Her mother, Mary Stout, had rushed to her daughter's side and she fiercely guarded the body of her child from prying eyes and wagging tongues. Within hours of Sarah's death the gossips of Hertford were out in force: *Sarah has killed herself*, they whispered behind their hands, and worse, they said she was with child. Accusations of pregnancy and suicide would have been enough to ruin the reputation of any young woman in English society, but it was especially damaging to a family of Quakers who, as a religious minority, were daily subjected to censure and denigration. Once the coroner arrived he held a brief and barely perfunctory inquest which found that Sarah's death was a *non compos mentis* suicide. The coroner and his jurymen believed that in a moment of madness, possibly driven by a hysteria brought about by pregnancy, Sarah had thrown herself into the River Lea and drowned. In life Sarah had been a bright, well-loved and respectable member of the local community; by the coroner's verdict she was recast as a harlot and suicidal lunatic.

This was too much for Sarah's mother to bear. Her daughter's life had been cruelly snatched away and her memory tainted by 'awful lies and gossip'. Mary was desperate to prove that her daughter had not been disgraced and that she was not pregnant. Nothing could bring Sarah back, but Mary still hoped to restore to her daughter the dignity of her good reputation. Six weeks after Sarah's death, on 28 April, Mary arranged for her daughter's body to be exhumed and a post-mortem conducted to prove that Sarah had not been pregnant. Surgeons had been sent for, although they attended the summons with a great deal of reluctance and tried to talk Mary out of her plan. A post-mortem six weeks after death, they advised, would reveal very little. The organs contained within Sarah's abdomen would be so rotten that it would be 'impossible to discover the uterus from the other parts'. If she were opened the surgeons would not be able to tell whether she had been pregnant 'unless the infant was become bony'. It seemed a hopeless endeavour, yet Mary was in a rage and demanded that the surgeons proceed. Resigned to their task, they prepared their instruments, unsealed the coffin and began their post-mortem on the body of Sarah Stout.

Upon opening the coffin the surgeons saw that Sarah's head, neck and shoulders were completely black and corrupted by rot, and once again they baulked at the prospect of conducting a post-mortem on a body that was so badly decomposed. 'However,' they later recalled, 'her mother would have it done, and so we did open her.' It seemed that Mary stood nearby, and flew into a rage whenever the surgeons hesitated. Having been given their orders the surgeons commenced their task. They noted that Sarah's abdomen was exceedingly bloated, and when they opened her they were shocked to discover that her organs were not, as they had suspected, in an advanced state of decay. In fact they seemed to be remarkably well preserved. Marvelling at this unexpected discovery, the surgeons set aside Sarah's guts and removed her uterus for closer inspection. They cut it open and observed that 'if there had been any thing there as minute as a hair, we might have seen it'. They unanimously agreed that Sarah had not been pregnant, and to Mary's enormous relief they signed an affidavit confirming her daughter's virginity.

The primary objective of the post-mortem was complete, yet the surgeons were intrigued by the fair condition of Sarah's organs. In their experience the stomach, intestines and lungs of a drowned victim should have decomposed within a few weeks, and by their measure Sarah's organs should not have been so well preserved. To satisfy their professional curiosity they decided to examine Sarah a little further. They made an incision into the bloated stomach where 'it sunk flat, and let out wind', and to their astonishment they saw that it was empty of any water. Next they opened the breast and the lobes of the lungs before moving on to examine the diaphragm, each of which they were equally shocked to discover were 'all dry'. They rolled Sarah on to her side and noted that the interior of the coffin was also completely dry. Dr Coatsworth, one of the surgeons, remarked to the others: 'This woman could not be drowned, for if she had taken in water, the water must have rotted all the guts.' The majority of the surgeons agreed that Sarah showed no internal signs of drowning, and concluded that she must have been dead before entering into the water. This was a shocking discovery that contradicted the coroner's verdict of death by drowning. Sarah, they believed, had not killed herself. This left the awful possibility that she had, in fact, been murdered. But by whom? At once all eyes turned on the last person to have seen her alive on the night she died: Spencer Cowper.

Spencer was the second son of Sir William Cowper, 2nd Baronet, of Hertfordshire. He had received his education at Westminster, and afterwards he studied law at Middle Temple where he distinguished himself as a principled and dedicated student, although he was occasionally rebellious and clashed with the Inns' administrative authorities. At twenty-nine years old he was a successful barrister working out of London. Like Sarah's, his father was a dedicated Whig politician, and it was through politics that the Cowper and Stout families were acquainted. They often dined together in Hertford to discuss their strategies for local elections, and it was at social events such as these that Sarah and Spencer had first met. Spencer was a handsome and desirable man, successful in his business and reportedly fierce in court. He was well married and his friends, who were themselves prominent men in both Hertfordshire and London, held him to be a good, honest man who was above reproach. It seemed unlikely to the citizens of Hertford that such a respectable and well-liked man as Spencer could have laid violent hands upon young Sarah, and yet that is precisely what Mary Stout accused him of doing. She believed that Spencer was no gentleman, but was instead a cold-blooded killer. Armed with the evidence revealed by the post-mortem and the fact that Spencer was the last person to be seen with Sarah, Mary pressed to have him arrested and put on trial for murder.

Spencer languished in prison for two months while the prosecution built their case against him. Alongside Spencer three other men had been accused of being his accomplices. They were Ellis Stephens, a legal clerk; William Rogers, a steward of the King's Bench; and John Marson, an attorney in Southwark. All the accused were legal professionals and as such they understood the dire profundity of their situation: a guilty verdict would see them hanged. Between them they decided that Spencer, a battle-hardened barrister who had many times defended clients in Hertford's assize courts, would be their representative. Although confined in prison, Spencer had not been idle and from his cell he orchestrated his defence strategy. It was not easy, and Spencer felt the weight of responsibility upon his shoulders as his friends relied on him to save them from the hangman's noose. He had but one chance, and almost no time to convince a jury of their innocence, for murder trials in this period were conducted at breakneck speed and were expected to be wrapped up in just a few short hours. Spencer's defence strategy had to be swift and sure, leaving the jury without a shadow of a doubt that he and his friends were innocent of murder.

At last the touring courts of assizes had arrived in Hertford, and with it came Judge Baron Henry Hatsell from the central courts. It was his role to pass judgment on civil and criminal cases deemed too severe to be dealt with by the local courts. The impending trial of Spencer Cowper was big news and the Shire Hall, Hertford's dedicated session house, was filled to bursting with families, friends, neighbours and rivals – all of them keen to see one of Hertford's brightest, and by now most notorious, men stand trial for his life. Reporters from the presses sat poised with their notebooks, ready to record every word in shorthand for later publication. The early modern public were fascinated by the drama of murder trials, and transcripts of high-profile cases such as Spencer's sold like hot cakes. Excitement hummed through the courtroom, and the noise was at times so loud that it was impossible to hear a single word clearly spoken. Legal clerks and court administrators shuffled their papers, fiddled with their stationery and whispered in anticipation. Material witnesses stood just outside the courtroom, nervously awaiting the commencement of the trial and their call to enter the fray. Standing at the bar were the four accused prisoners: Spencer Cowper, Ellis Stevens, William Rogers and John Marson. They were all old hands of the courtroom and as such exuded an air of composure that was not typical of those who found themselves in similar surroundings. Opposite them stood the prosecuting council, Mr Jones, who was impatient for the trial to begin.

Judge Baron Hatsell signalled his readiness to start proceedings, and a hush descended on the courtroom. The clerk of arraignment stepped forward and instructed each of the accused to raise their hand before he proceeded to read the indictment. The prosecution held that on the 13th day of March 1699, Spencer Cowper violently attacked Sarah Stout, and with the help of John Marson, Ellis Stephens and William Rogers tied a rope about her neck and 'by the squeezing and griping of the neck and throat' did strangle, kill and murder her. The accused then attempted to hide her body by casting it into the river.

The clerk of arraignment turned to Spencer and said, 'How sayest thou, Spencer Cowper, art thou guilty of the felony and murder whereof thou standest indicted, or not guilty?'

'Not guilty,' Spencer replied.

The other three defendants likewise pleaded not guilty.

With the indictments read and pleas given, Mr Jones began his opening statement wherein he detailed to the jury the prosecution's version of events on the night that Sarah Stout died. Monday, 13 March was the first day of the previous assizes, when the touring circuit court had arrived in Hertford. As was his custom, Spencer had travelled from London to follow the court in the hope that he could solicit profitable cases. When the assizes were in town Hertford's already thriving inns and taverns were fit to bursting.

Spencer, anticipating a rush on accommodation, had wisely booked his room in advance at an establishment belonging to a Mr Barefoot. The weather that day had been exceedingly wet and dreary, and having just arrived in Hertford Spencer checked into his room and remained there for some time to dry off and recover after his long journey. Unbeknown to Spencer, his wife back in London had written a letter to their mutual friend Sarah Stout in which she inferred that Spencer would possibly lodge with her at her house just outside town. Upon hearing of this mix-up, and already settled in his room at Mr Barefoot's, Spencer intended to see Sarah later to clear up any misunderstandings relating to his accommodation in Hertford.

At approximately 2 p.m. Spencer visited Sarah and her mother Mary at their house, and there they dined together until 4 p.m. At this time Spencer excused himself, saying that he had to leave on some business; however, he promised to return to have supper and lodge the night with the Stouts after all. Whatever obligation Spencer had to Mr Barefoot seemed to have been put aside in favour of accepting Sarah's invitation to stay. Later that evening Spencer returned to the Stouts and he kept good company with Sarah until approximately 11 p.m., when Sarah told the maid, Miss Walker, to prepare Spencer's room. Miss Walker did as she was instructed: she set a pan of heated coals in Spencer's bed and then waited for him to come upstairs so she could get him settled in his room. Yet Spencer did not come, and at 11.15 p.m. Miss Walker was surprised to hear the loud 'clap' of the front door closing. Wondering at the meaning of the noise, she went downstairs, to discover that both Spencer and Sarah were gone. Worried at this unusual turn of events, Miss Walker fetched Mary Stout, and together they sat and waited for Sarah to return to the house; yet Sarah never came home.

That same night John Marson, Ellis Stephens and William Rogers were lodging in town at an establishment called Gurrey's. They sat together all night by a fire, drinking and talking loudly in full view of the staff and other patrons. They chatted about work, and other subjects that interested men halfway into their cups, and in short time their discourse fell upon the subject of Sarah Stout. One of the men bawdily asked Marson if Sarah was not an old sweetheart of his. 'Aye,' Marson replied with some dudgeon, 'but she cast me off!' They drank more, laughed raucously and speculated as to the romantic adventures of the lovely young Sarah. Marson, clearly smarting over the memory of his rejection, darkly remarked that 'By this time a friend of mine has done her business.' Later on one of the party was also overheard saying that 'Sarah Stout's courting days are over'. The staff at Gurrey's who listened to these crass comments concerning a respectable young woman and devout Quaker wondered at their meaning. When Sarah's body was discovered the following morning the men's drunken banter of the night before was considered to have held a far more sinister meaning.

Mr Jones summarised to the jury the basis for the prosecution's case against Spencer Cowper: 'Mr Cowper was the last man unfortunately in her company; I could wish it had not been so with all my heart; it is a very unfortunate thing.' Spencer and Sarah had together gone out of the house and into the dark of night, and from there she was never seen alive again. That same evening Spencer's friends had been overheard making ominous comments concerning Sarah, comments that suggested foreknowledge of her death. After Sarah's body had been found the next morning Spencer and his three friends met in town, and quickly left Hertford. It was suspicious, Mr Jones opined, that Spencer, a friend of the Stout family, did not make any effort to see Sarah's body or offer any condolences to her grieving mother before he hastened back to London.

Spencer was not impressed by the prosecution's case, and scoffed that he had been brought to trial on the basis of such flimsy circumstantial evidence. Addressing the jury, he said: 'I did not in the least imagine that so little . . . could possibly have affected me to so great a degree as to bring me to this place to answer for the worst fact that the worst of men could be guilty of.' Furthermore, Spencer stressed that there was no murder to be answered for, since

Sarah had clearly killed herself in a fit of madness. And what of this nonsenses about a rope? The prosecution, he argued, had no evidence to show that Sarah had been strangled, as they claimed. 'There is not a syllable of proof,' he said to the jury, 'at most, it amounts to make us suspect a murder, not proved, but only suspected.' It was not enough for the prosecution to imply a murder may have been committed; they had to prove it.

Mr Jones was well aware that the case outlined so far in his opening statement to the jury was largely circum-stantial. This was a problem he confronted head-on: 'The gentlemen at the bar stand accused of one of the foulest and most wicked crimes almost that any man can remember,' he said, 'for here is a young gentlewoman of this county strangled and murdered in the night time. The thing was done in the dark, therein the evidence cannot be so plain as otherwise might be.' In making this statement Mr Jones was preparing the jury for the extraordinary body of evidence that was to immediately follow. There were no witnesses to say what had happened that night, and so the prosecution's case hinged upon proving that Sarah had not committed suicide. If he could prove this, then the only explanation left was that she had been murdered, and by the process of elimination the only plausible suspect was Spencer Cowper. Mr Jones made clear to the jury the direction of his case: 'We have here, in a manner, two trials; one to acquit the party that is dead, and to satisfy the world, and to vindicate her reputation, that she did not murder herself, but she was murdered by other hands.' To prove Spencer's guilt, Mr Jones first had to prove Sarah's innocence.

The first witness called to the stand was the maid, Miss Walker. She had been the last person to have seen Sarah and Spencer together, and she claimed that she heard them both leaving the house. It was her evidence at the inquest that identified Spencer as the last person to be seen with Sarah before she died, thus making him the prime suspect for her murder. That day in court she recounted one more time how she went upstairs to ready Spencer's room, and afterwards heard the front door closing: 'I went up to do as the clock struck eleven, and in about a quarter of an hour, I heard the door shut.' She then recalled that she and her mistress Mary Stout sat up all night waiting for Sarah to return. Keen to undermine Miss Walker's testimony, Spencer asked her, 'Pray will you recollect a little, and be very particular, as to the time when I went out at night.' 'Sir,' she answered, 'it was a quarter after eleven by our clock; the difference between the town clock and ours was half an hour.'

'But you say by your clock it was a quarter after eleven?'

'Yes sir,' she replied.

Judge Baron Hatsell interjected at this moment to ask, 'Which clock was earliest, yours or the town clock?'

'Ours was half an hour faster than theirs,' she said.

This back and forth about the house clock and the town clock was significant, for when Miss Walker testified that she heard the front door slam closed at 11.15 p.m. by her clock, it was in fact 10.45 p.m.

This was a piece of testimony that Spencer used to his advantage. 'In point of time,' he said to the jury, 'I shall prove it utterly impossible I could be guilty of the fact I am accused of.' On the night of Sarah's death, as the town clock was striking 11. p.m., Spencer said that he had been seen by several witnesses at the Glove and Dolphin inn in town. To prove this he called to the stand Elizabeth Spurr, who was working in the Glove and Dolphin on the night in question.

'Do you remember my coming to your house, and at what time?' Spencer asked her.

'The clock struck eleven, just as you came into the door,' she said.

'How long did I stay at the Glove?'

'About a quarter of an hour.'

'How far is it from the Glove and Dolphin to Mrs Stout's house?' he asked.

'About a quarter of a mile,' she replied.

Next Spencer went on to explain to the jury that after he had settled his business at the Glove and Dolphin he returned to his lodgings at Barefoot's. To prove this he called several members of the Barefoot family to testify that they had seen him coming into their house at just after 11 p.m. and that he had retired to his room, from which he did not emerge for the remainder of the night.

The prosecution would have the jury believe that Spencer had left Sarah Stout's house at 10.45. p.m, killed her, thrown her in the river and then walked to the Glove and Dolphin in time for the town clock to strike 11 p.m. This meant that the whole crime would have had to have been committed within fifteen minutes. To prove that this was impossible Spencer called upon several respectable members of the community who had conducted experiments as to how long it took them to walk from Sarah's house to the river, then onwards to the Glove and Dolphin. 'I would observe to your Lordship,' Spencer addressed Judge Baron Hatsell, 'that to go from Mrs Stout's house to the place where she was drowned, and to return from thence to the Glove and Dolphin, will take up at least half an hour, as I shall prove.' Sir William Ashurst, who had conducted his own experiment, was called to take the stand. 'My Lord,' Ashurst spoke to the judge, 'I cannot say I walked as fast as I could . . . I walked as people usually do, and I found it took up half an hour and a minute.'

This evidence was backed up by his friend Mr Thompson, who said, 'I walked it before . . . My Lord, indeed it would take a complete half-hour.'

Another witness who had conducted the same walking

experiment said it took him upwards of forty-five minutes to complete the journey. Spencer concluded that it would have been impossible for him to have left the Stouts' house at 10.45 p.m., completed the crime and walked to the Glove and Dolphin by 11 p.m. It was far more likely, Spencer told the jury, that Miss Walker was an unreliable witness who was 'not so cautious and careful how she swears, as I think she ought to be'.

The prosecution, sensing this particular battle had been lost, quickly moved the focus of the trial on to the discovery of Sarah Stout's body and the post-mortem examination that was carried out six weeks after her death. She was the victim, but she was also the main body of evidence upon which the prosecution had hung their entire case. To counter the prosecution's bold new strategy the defence too had summoned their own expert witnesses. What followed in court was an intensely adversarial and at times bizarre affair in which both the prosecution and the defence called upon legal and medical experts in order to assert their version of the truth. Never before in English legal history had forensic evidence been so prominently used in a court of law, and those lucky enough to cram themselves into the courtroom to bear witness were shocked and amazed by the unprecedented proceedings. These were the early years of the Enlightenment, and professionals in the medico-legal sphere were becoming increasingly aware of the value of evidence based on facts, reason and experimentation. It was inevitable that advances in the fields of medicine and forensic pathology were to filter down into the realm of criminal law.

Mr Jones first wanted to prove to the jury that Sarah had not been drowned. This was not easy, and even today the diagnosis of death by drowning is extremely difficult; while there are several external and internal symptoms that are indicative of 'true' drowning, they are nonetheless broadly inconsistent and subject to a great number of physiological and environmental factors. Simply put, when a body is recovered from water there is no one sign that a modern forensic pathologist can point to as a certain diagnosis of death by drowning. However, since antiquity it had been historically understood that drowned bodies typically displayed one of the following immediate symptoms: it was understood that bodies whose lungs had been voided of all air sank when submerged in water; the stomachs of drowned victims were expected to have been bloated or 'swelled' with swallowed water; and lastly, bodies recovered from the water sometimes purged white foam from the nose and mouth. Mr Jones hoped to show the jury that since Sarah's body did not display these symptoms, then she could not have been drowned.

James Berry, the mill owner who was the first to discover Sarah's body, was called to the stand.

'When you found her,' Mr Jones said to Berry, 'do you remember, how, in what manner she was found?'

'Yes,' Berry replied. 'I saw something a floating in the water, so I went out to see what it was, and I saw a part of her clothes.'

'Did you see her face?'

'No, not then.'

'How much was she under water, do you conceive?' Mr Jones asked. 'She might be under water about five or six inches,' Berry answered.

'Then her whole body was not under water, was it?'

'Yes,' Berry said, indicating that although Sarah's body was partially submerged under a few inches of water, it was nonetheless floating near the surface and was clearly visible in some parts above the waterline. Mr Jones was keen to establish this fact to the jury, as according to contemporary medical knowledge drowned bodies were expected to sink completely, all the way to the bottom. A body that was floating close to the surface was assumed to have had air in the lungs. Mr Jones pressed onwards with this line of questioning:

'Was there any thing under her, in the water, to prevent her sinking?' he asked Berry.

'No,' Berry said. 'I do not know there was; she lay on her right side, and her right arm was driven between the stakes, which are within a foot of one another.' Here Berry was referring to the stakes that were nailed to the bridge where Sarah's body was found.

It appeared that Sarah's body had been driven into the stakes by the force of the water running to the mills. By now the jury must have been wondering if her right arm, caught between the stakes, was what prevented her body from sinking all the way beneath the surface. Mr Jones feared that the stakes would undermine his theory that Sarah floated because she had air in her lungs, and so he called a further ten witnesses – maids, servants and working folk who had been nearby when Berry made his gruesome discovery – who each testified that they believed Sarah's body was floating independently of the stakes. Mr Jones pointedly asked them the same question:

'Did any thing hinder her from sinking?'

'Neither stakes nor any thing there,' came the repeated reply.

With each successive witness, Mr Jones hoped to prove beyond any doubt that Sarah's body was not being held at the surface by the stakes. She floated, he maintained, because her lungs were dry.

In reply Spencer summoned his own witnesses to speak on the subject of Sarah's body as it lay in the water. In a move that was to typify a great deal of Spencer's defence strategy, his witnesses were deliberately selected to undermine the credibility of those of the prosecution. Mr Jones had relied on the testimonies of maids, servants, passers-by and rubberneckers while Spencer called to the stand the civic officials who, by the order of the coroner, had personally removed Sarah's body from the water. Robert Dew, a parish officer, testified that Sarah's body had been firmly wedged between the stakes: 'She lay on her right side, her head rather downwards; and as they pulled her up, I cried "Hold, hold hold, you hurt her arm"; and so they kneeled down and took her arm away from the stakes . . . they could not have got her out else.' According to Dew, Sarah's arm was so tightly caught between the stakes that she could not be moved unless she was untangled first. Spencer then called Mr Young, a constable who also assisted in the removal of Sarah's body from the water. Young too testified that Sarah's body was tightly caught between the stakes: 'She laid sideway, that he could not take her up till they had let her down again, and so they twisted her out sideway; for the stakes were so near together she could not lie upon her belly or her back.' With the testimonies of just two witnesses Spencer had cast doubt upon the great volume of evidence that had been given on behalf of the prosecution.

The prosecution next moved to focus on the condition of Sarah's body after it had been removed from the water. Mr Jones called Leonard Dell to take the stand. Dell had helped to carry Sarah to the riverbank, and in doing so he had closely observed the condition of her body.

'We took her,' Dell explained, 'and carried her into the meadow just by, and laid her on the bank.'

Judge Baron Hatsell interjected to ask Dell, 'When you took her out . . . did you observe that any water was in her body?'

'None at all,' Dell replied, before adding, 'but there was some small matter of froth that came from her mouth and nostrils.'

This line of questioning was unplanned, and was not the sort of scrutiny that Mr Jones welcomed. Any mention of foam might steer the jury to think Sarah may have drowned.

'My Lord!' A juryman called out, further interrupting Mr Jones's examination. 'I desire to know whether her stays were laced?'

'Yes, she was laced,' Dell responded. Tightly laced stays, a kind of rigid corset, may have prevented water from being forced into the stomach or at the very least hidden signs of swelling.

Spencer, sensing an opportunity to wrestle control of this witness away from Mr Jones, jumped into the fray to ask, 'If I take you right, you say she was straight laced?'

'Her stays were laced,' Dell confirmed.

'And you say there was froth and foam came out of her mouth and nostrils?'

'Yes sir,' Dell said.

Without another word Spencer sat back down, pleased

that Mr Jones's mismanagement of his witness had only served to strengthen the defence's position.

Mr Jones then moved to discuss the examination of Sarah's body after it had been relocated to the privacy of a nearby barn. The prosecution's professional witnesses were those surgeons who had first examined Sarah's body. The lead surgeon, Mr Dimsdale Jr, was the first called to take the stand. Yet before Mr Jones opened his mouth to pose his first question, Spencer interrupted him. 'My Lord,' he called loudly to the judge, 'if your lordship pleases, I have some physicians of note and eminency that are come down from London; I desire that they be called into court to hear what the surgeons say.' Spencer then theatrically called for ten graduate physicians to enter the courtroom, several of whom were well-known public figures, including the famed anatomist Dr William Cowper, and Dr Samuel Garth, who was a lecturer on respiration at the Royal College of Physicians.

The eyes of the jury were fixed upon these eminent physicians as they trooped single-file into the courtroom before they snapped back to the solitary figure of Dimsdale as he stood rigid on the witness stand. 'You are a physician, I suppose sir?' Judge Baron Hatsell pointedly asked Dimsdale. The witness was forced to reply that he was only 'a surgeon, My Lord'. The contrast in both professional status and competence between the surgeon Dimsdale and the ten graduate physicians who stood firmly on the side of the defence was intended to be embarrassingly stark. Physicians were university-educated professionals with a wealth of medical training, while surgeons had little or no formal education and were mainly linked to the trade guild of the Barber-Surgeons. Before Dimsdale was able to speak a single word, his professional expertise had already been soundly undermined.

Mr Jones asked Dimsdale to give an account of the condition of Sarah's body.

'I found a little swelling on the side of her neck, and she was black on both sides, and more particularly on the left side, and between her breasts and up towards the collar bone,' Dimsdale said.

'How were her ears?' Jones asked.

'There was a settling of blood on both sides of the neck, that was all I saw at the time.'

These black marks, the prosecution argued, signified that deadly violence had been inflicted upon Sarah. Mr Jones was especially interested in the bruising about her neck, claiming that this was the mark left by Spencer when he allegedly strangled Sarah with a piece of rope. Spencer, however, had another theory. He asked Dimsdale to recall the evidence he himself had given at the coroner's inquest, in which he testified that the marks were no more than 'a common stagnation' of blood that was 'usual in dead bodies'.

This settling of the blood, otherwise known as *livor mortis* or lividity, is the gravitational pooling of blood in bodies and manifests as a deep-red or purple discolouration on the skin. Strange that Dimsdale would suppose these marking to be natural phenomena during the inquest, but signs of murder once he was on the witness stand in court. Spencer's theory was supported by another witness, who described the discolouration as being 'reddish and blackish as to colour . . . like a settling of blood'. Testimony heard earlier in the trial had described Sarah as lying in the water with her head facing downwards, and so it was entirely possible for blood to have settled around her head, neck and collarbone. Spencer pressed Dimsdale to recall once again what he had said during the inquest, to which Dimsdale angrily replied, 'I do not remember a word of it.'

'Had she any circle about her neck?' Spencer asked, questioning whether there was a telltale ligature mark round Sarah's neck.

'No,' Dimsdale was forced to reply, 'not upon my oath.'

The next witness called to the stand was Sarah Peppercorn, a midwife. Midwives were considered authorities in pregnancy, childbirth and female physiology and were often relied upon by the courts and coroners to act as expert witnesses. After Sarah's body had been examined in the barn, it was later carried up to her house and placed under the care of women, including Mrs Peppercorn. The women were horrified to see that Sarah's body had been delivered to them naked and in an 'indecent manner'. They wrapped her in a sheet and shielded her from public view, yet there in the courtroom these female witnesses had no choice but to unwrap Sarah for the scrutiny of men. Judge Baron Hatsell asked Mrs Peppercorn why she in particular had been asked examine Sarah Stout.

'To knew if she was with child,' she told the judge, 'for it was reported she had drowned herself because she was with child.' Mrs Peppercorn described how Mary Stout had summoned her to examine Sarah in order to prove that she was not pregnant. 'I was sent for to give an account whether she was or not [with child], and I found she was not.'

'Did you observe how her body was?' Mr Jones asked.

'Her body was very well as any woman's should be,' she replied haughtily, unwilling to expose Sarah any more than necessary.

The next witness was Elizabeth Hustler, who had helped to clean Sarah's body. Mr Jones asked her:

'Had you the view of the body . . . the day you heard she was drowned?'

'She was not drowned, My Lord!' Hustler cried, exposing Mr Jones's unfortunate slip. 'Her body was very lank and thin,' she added, 'and no water appeared to be in it.'

'Was there any water about her mouth and nose?' Mr Jones asked.

'Not when I saw her.'

Next came Ann Pilkinton, who said: 'The next day Mrs Stout sent for me again, to put on her daughter's shrowd, and I was the one that helped to draw the sheet away, and there was not one drop of water come from her. I laid a cloth under her chin, when I helped her into the coffin, but I did not see the least moisture from her.' By this testimony Mr Jones wanted to show that Sarah's body was dry and lacked the expected signs of drowning.

The lack of water in Sarah's body was a point that underpinned the prosecution's entire case against Spencer. Mr Jones was confident in his ability to prove Sarah had not been drowned, yet he struggled to connect the forensic evidence to an act of murder, specifically murder by strangulation. This became uncomfortably evident during his questioning of another surgeon, Dr Coatsworth. During his testimony Coatsworth began by describing his examination of Sarah's uterus, then the absence of water in her stomach, lungs and diaphragm and finally the surprising lack of putrefaction in her intestines, stomach and lungs. Concerning signs of violence reportedly seen about her head and neck, Coatsworth stated:

'It was impossible for us to discover . . . because they were so rotten.'

'Did you make an incision into those parts of the neck and head?' Mr Jones asked.

'No,' Coatsworth replied. 'I told Mrs Stout and her son, if you imagine the skull to be injured, I will open the head . . . they said they did not expect a broken skull . . . and so we did not examine it.'

The renowned physician Dr Garth was incredulous. 'If these gentlemen had found a cord, or the print of it about the neck of this unfortunate gentlewoman, or any wound that had occasioned her death, they might have said something.' In truth the post-mortem had not been intended to prove the cause of Sarah's death, but only to exonerate her from a charge of pregnancy. Yet it seemed extraordinary to Dr Garth that as soon as murder was suspected, the surgeons present had not attempted to discover how she was killed.

The next witness called was the surgeon Dr Dimsdale Sr (the father of Dr Dimsdale Jr), who had also participated in the post-mortem.

'Give your reasons, why you believed she was not drowned,' Mr Jones directed his witness.

'We found no water in her,' Dimsdale Sr explained, 'her intestines were not putrefied; for if there had been water in her, that would have caused a fermentation, and that would have rotted the guts.'

Judge Baron Hatsell interrupted the examination to ask: 'Could you tell, so many weeks after, whether she was drowned or no?'

This was a question that intrigued many in the court-room as they had never encountered a case in which the duration between death and post-mortem had been so long. Dimsdale Sr was confident in his reply:

'Yes My Lord, for this reason . . . if there had been a pint of water, it would have rotted her lights and her guts; and that is done in a week's time by fermentation.'

'Did you ever see a body that was drowned, opened six weeks after?' Spencer challenged.

'No, never,' Dimsdale Sr replied.

Spencer then called one of his own witnesses, the physician Dr Morley, to give his opinion as to the lack of water in Sarah's body. 'There is no absolute necessity that she should have a great quantity of water in her,' Dr Morley explained; 'if this gentlewoman did voluntarily drown herself, she then, in all likelihood, threw herself into the water with a resolution of keeping her breath for a speedy suffocation; and then if upon the first endeavours of respiration she drew into her lungs two ounces of water, it was the same thing to drowning of her as if there had been two ton.' Dr Morley explained that a person might drown on little as two ounces of water. To prove this to the court he had conducted several experiments on dogs: 'We last night drowned a dog, and afterwards dissected him, and found not a spoonful of water in his stomach, and I believe about two ounces in his lungs.' He had then drowned a second dog, and again found very little water inside the body, along with a quantity of foam purging from the dog's nose and mouth.

This was the daring and exciting new science that was emerging during the seventeenth century, and, as barbaric as those experiments may seem today, they were nonetheless foundational in the development of forensic science. Here, for perhaps the first time in English legal history, empirical evidence played a major role in a murder trial. The physician Dr Gelstrop continued these experiments on dogs when he simulated Sarah's alleged murder by hanging a spaniel, before throwing its corpse into a body of water. The poor creature floated, leading Dr Gelstrop to believe that the dog's long hair helped to buoy its body. He then hanged a short-haired breed of dog and observed that its corpse sank immediately. The outcome of these rather gruesome experiments demonstrated to the court that hanged bodies of dogs who had succumbed to a 'dry death' on land may both sink or float when thrown into water. This evidence not only cast doubt on the prosecution's insistence that drowned bodies must sink, it also challenged the accepted symptoms of death by drowning. Blind acceptance of long-held beliefs was no longer sufficient, and those men working in the medico-legal sphere were encouraged to test the validity of ancient wisdom through science and experimentation.

Spencer was well aware of the power of the evidence put forward by the physicians, and he continued this line of questioning by calling Dr Morley back to the stand.

'Do you think, doctor,' Spencer asked, 'it is to be known six weeks after if a person is drowned?'

'I think it is morally impossible,' Morley replied. As to the lack of any water observed during the post-mortem, this was easily explained: 'We see in persons that die of dropsies, that the water will work itself out before it is buried . . . where the water lies in the stomach and guts [it] had nothing to hinder its working out when it ferments.'

Another physician, coincidentally named Dr Cowper (no relation to Spencer Cowper), testified: 'It is so commonly known, that the contents in the stomach of a dead body are discharged . . . fluid must be forced from them six weeks after death.' The matter of the extent of the putre-faction of Sarah's body was also hotly debated, with Dr Garth explaining to the court that rates of decomposition can be affected by all manner of conditions. The accelerated decomposition of the head, neck and arm was likely caused by the *livor mortis* that had been observed on her body when she was pulled from the water, and the lack of decom-position elsewhere may have been affected by many things, such as the lack of water in her body, the climate and weather, the state of the coffin and the contents of her stomach and intestines when she died. To make a diagnosis of drowning based upon the rate of decomposition was, according to Dr Morley, utterly impossible.

That a man should be accused of murder on the basis of so little evidence was unconscionable. Spencer was outraged, and insisted that the prosecution could 'neither prove the murder in general, nor that [we the accused] did it in particular'. He angrily resented the untold damage that had been caused to his personal and professional reputation. Spencer believed the trial to be a sham, orchestrated by the political enemies of his family. Yet he was not the only person to have suffered so much public shame. Throughout the trial Sarah's body had been metaphorically laid out, stripped, opened and examined in excruciating forensic detail. For her family, who sat silently in the courtroom, it must have been an agonising ordeal, yet they still had more to endure as a furious Spencer now went on the attack.

To save himself and his three fellow defendants from the hangman's noose, Spencer had to prove beyond a shadow of doubt that Sarah had committed suicide. This truly was a trial of two murders, for to clear his own name Spencer was forced to implicate Sarah as a self-murderer, and in doing so utterly ruin her good name. 'Perhaps,' Spencer addressed the jury, 'it may be said, that in honour I ought to conceal the weakness of this gentlewoman; but then, in honour and justice is these gentlemen that are falsely accused with me, I cannot do it.' He was fighting for his life and for the lives of his friends; he could not hold back. At this juncture the focus of the trial shifted away from Spencer and fell upon Sarah, who in death was unable to speak a single word in her defence.

'It is almost a certainty,' Spencer argued, 'that she was the cause of her own death.' But why would Sarah take her own life? She was prosperous, well liked and a woman of good moral standing in her community; a jury in this period would find it hard to imagine why such a successful and popular person would wish to harm themselves. Yet Spencer was to reveal to the court a scandalous tale in which Sarah's motives were presented as those of a madwoman and a lovesick fool.

Spencer's first witness in this matter was Mr Bowd, a merchant tailor who owned a fabric shop in town. Sarah was both a loyal customer and a friend to Mr Bowd. Spencer asked his witness to recall an episode that had happened twelve months ago. Mr Bowd and Sarah had been sitting together discussing business when he was struck by her wan countenance and sombre disposition.

'What is the matter with you?' he had asked her. 'There is something more than ordinary; you seem melancholy.'

'You are come from London,' she had replied, referring to his recent business trip to the capital, 'and you have heard something or other.' She must have been alluding to whatever gossip was doing the rounds in London's merchant community, in particular gossip about herself.

'I believe you are in love,' Mr Bowd teased.

'In love!' she cried, taking hold of his hand. 'Truly, I must confess it; but I did not think I would be guilty of such folly.'

'I admire that should make you uneasy,' he said, seeming deeply concerned by her apparent unhappiness. He sought to offer her some advice: 'If you love him, make him happy, and yourself easy.'

Sarah was unmarried and free to take a husband, yet she baulked at the suggestion.

'That cannot be,' she replied sadly, 'the world shall not say I changed my religion for a husband.' She was a Quaker, and was not permitted to marry outside her religion.

This forbidden love, Mr Bowd surmised, must have been the wellspring of her unhappiness. Some time later, Sarah returned to visit Mr Bowd at his shop to pay for some fabric she had purchased at an earlier date.

He had cheerfully asked her, 'How do you like it? Have you made it up yet?'

'No,' she replied morosely, 'and I believe I shall never live to wear it.'

Spencer then called upon several of Sarah's female friends and acquaintances to recall their memories of her melancholic temperament. A Mrs Bendy testified that Sarah was 'so troubled with melancholy that she could not tell what to do with herself', adding that 'it disordered her so, she said that she would rather have chosen sickness than so much disorder in her mind'. Another friend, Mrs Low, told the court, 'She often complained to me, that she was very melancholy and uneasy.' She remembered a time when they had been walking in a field together, when Mrs Low asked Sarah why she seemed so unhappy: 'She told me it was a secret; but she said she lived a very melancholy life. I am apt to believe you are in love!' Mrs Low had cried, observing in Sarah that particular kind of sadness unique to lovesickness. Sarah admitted so, and lamented that her love was indeed a secret, one 'that would end her days'. Her other friends and servants testified that Sarah often lay in bed for days on end, that she suffered from chronic headaches and resented her own religion for making her an outcast in love. On one occasion Sarah had confided to a friend that she thought about drowning herself.

Who was this love that had caused Sarah so much suffering? The secret that Sarah had protected so closely in life was about to be revealed to all. Spencer had in his possession a number of private letters written by Sarah; letters that would identify her secret love. The first letter, dated September 1697, was addressed to Spencer's friend Thomas Marshall. Spencer had introduced the pair, and Marshall had fancied himself a potential suitor for Sarah, although he was the first to admit he was disastrously unskilled when it came to the art of wooing. The couple briefly courted that summer, although Marshall's interest had run hotter than Sarah's, whose letters were playful yet cool. She signed her first letter 'your loving duck'; however, she subsequently refused Marshall when he pressed for her hand in marriage. Spencer then recalled to the court an episode in which he and Sarah had been walking together soon after she had rejected Marshall. She scolded Spencer for trying to play the matchmaker.

'Mr Cowper,' she chided him, 'I did not think you had been so dull . . . did you imagine I intended to marry Mr Marshall?'

Spencer was taken aback, and replied that he thought that she did.

'No,' she said, 'I thought it might serve to divert the censure of the world, and favour our acquittance.'

Her courtship with Marshall had been no more than a ruse to get closer to her true heart's desire. Sarah had been in love with Spencer.

What followed, according to Spencer, was a troublesome one-sided infatuation. Sarah wrote him desperate letters, lamenting how she suffered long nights and unhappy days due to his 'rocky heart' and unrelenting thoughtlessness regarding her tender feelings. She became so persistent that Spencer went to lengths to avoid her company. On one occasion Spencer heard news that Sarah had come to

London to seek him out, and in his desperation he hid from her. He told his friends to put it about that he was away on business in Deptford, and that he was not available to callers. Sarah had hoped to corner Spencer at a dinner engagement, but when she heard that he was away she bolted from the table and was seen falling into 'a woman's fit of swooning'. She afterwards pestered Spencer with even more letters, and begged him to come to her in Hertford where he could make her easy and relieve her suffering. On 9 March she wrote to him: 'Come life or death, I am resolved never to desert you' and begged Spencer once more to go to her house, with an invitation that he should cohabit with her: an invitation many interpreted to mean she had asked Spencer to leave his wife. At last he relented, and went to her on that fateful night of 13 March with the intention of ending the one-sided love affair once and for all.

The prosecution held that on the night in question Spencer had lost his temper, and in his desperation to be rid of Sarah he had strangled her with a rope. With the help of his friends he had then thrown her body into the River Lea. Spencer argued that Sarah had been driven mad by her love, and when confronted with his firm refusal she had fled the house and thrown herself into the river. After nine exhausting hours both the prosecution and the defence had rested their cases. This was quite possibly the longest trial Judge Baron Hatsell had ever endured, and as he summed up the proceedings he admitted that he was very tired, somewhat confused and 'a little faint'. He reminded the jury of the maid Sarah Walker's evidence and the discrepancies concerning the time in which the murder was supposed to have been committed, of the witnesses who spoke of Sarah's condition in the water and the expert testimonies of the surgeons and physicians on the symptoms of drowned bodies. Finally he reflected upon the evidence concerning Sarah Stout's private life, of her alleged lovesick melancholy and her infatuation with a man who was now accused of being her murderer.

'Gentlemen,' Judge Baron Hatsell concluded, 'I was very much puzzled in my thoughts, and was at a loss to find out what inducement there could be to draw in Mr Cowper, or these three other gentlemen, to commit such a horrid, barbarous murder. And on the other hand, I could not imagine what there should be to induce this gentlewoman, a person of plentiful fortune, and a very sober good reputation, to destroy herself. Well then,' he signalled to the jury, 'go together, and consider your evidence; and I pray God direct you in giving your verdict.' The jury retired, and in just half an hour they had reached their decision and returned to the courtroom. The murmuration of the crowd fell away to intense silence as all leaned forward in anticipation.

'Gentlemen,' the clerk of arraignment addressed the jury, 'how say you? Is he guilty of the felony and murder whereof he stands indicted, or not guilty?'

After so much had been said, in this one breathless moment the lives of four prosperous young men balanced upon this single question.

The foreman stood and delivered the jury's verdict: 'Not guilty.'

The verdict was explosive, and the trial became an overnight sensation throughout England. The pressmen, who had recorded every word, rushed to publish their transcripts and satiate the public's voracious curiosity for sensational murder trials. Spencer and his three friends had been acquitted, yet the fate of Sarah Stout remained an unsolved mystery; a mystery that armchair detectives and amateur sleuths fell upon with relish. Letters and pamphlets hotly debating the evidence presented in court circulated far and wide, and fictional accounts of the trial playfully theorised who or what had been responsible for Sarah's death. Many dogs had been sacrificed in the course of the trial, and many more were to be subjected to similar fates as the public attempted to recreate the experiments they read about in their true-crime pamphlets. And other strange experiments were to follow. The national newspaper *The Post Man* reported a public experiment that was witnessed by hundreds of spectators. In an attempt to recreate the conditions of Sarah's alleged murder, a hanged convict named William Ricles was dug out of his grave and flung into the river in the same spot where Sarah's body had been found. The mystery of what happened to Sarah Stout on that cold, wet night in March had captured the public imagination, and for centuries afterwards fans of true crime and historians alike puzzled over the details of her case in the hope of solving the mystery.

Throughout the trial Spencer had skilfully laid bare the weaknesses of the prosecution's case. From his prison cell he had orchestrated a defence strategy that centred empirical, forensic evidence and professional witness testimony that pushed to the sidelines evidence based upon mere supposition and speculation. Spencer was one of the first in English legal history to deploy this stratagem, and in doing so he changed how murder cases were investigated and prosecuted in the English courts. In staging such a robust defence he had wrought irrevocable damage upon Sarah's reputation, yet his hand had been forced: his life was in jeopardy and he had been compelled to fight his corner with a ruthlessness born of absolute necessity. Spencer emerged from his trial shaken but resolved to move forward in his life and to thrive in his legal career. At length he became a justice of the peace; however he was forever tainted by the scandal of his trial, and for years after the cry of 'Who killed the Quaker?' was often thrown at his back.

For Sarah's mother Mary, the trial was a bitter experience. From the moment her daughter's body had been found she fought tirelessly to restore Sarah's dignity and seek justice for her death. It was a cruel irony that in her attempt to restore her daughter's reputation she had exposed her to even more shame. Mary's religion meant that she was unable to swear an oath and could not speak in Sarah's defence during the trial, and so she had to sit in muted outrage as her daughter's alleged murderer focused the trial time and again upon Sarah's rumoured pregnancy, her lovesick infatuation with a married man, her inconstancy to her faith, and finally her alleged suicide. In its exacting focus on the circumstances of her death the trial had exposed faults in Sarah's character, and a deep sadness rooted in the loneliness of her heart. Yet these selective instances drawn from her final chapter did not define the whole of her life. Sarah had also been a successful, wealthy and well-liked young woman with an ambition to succeed in her business affairs. She maintained a great number of close friendships both within and without the Quaker community; she loved entertaining and parties, she enjoyed fashion and gossiping with her girlfriends, and underneath her proper exterior there beat a playful and rebellious heart. As the whole of England thrilled at the mystery of Sarah's death, those who knew her could at the very least comfort themselves with happier memories of her life.

NO MOTHER,
BUT A MONSTER

It was 1616 in the tranquil farming community of Acton, six miles outside London. The town's convenient proximity to the capital made it a popular summer retreat for London's courtiers, lawyers and wealthier classes. The industrious and idle rich alike were keen to escape the crush of the city's ever-expanding population, and so they flocked to East Acton and Friar's Place, where they built their grand holiday homes. There in Acton they could while away their summers in ease, and hope that the fresh air, bucolic surroundings and sweet mineral springs – the famed 'white waters' – would work restorative wonders upon body and soul. The taking of the waters had become a trend that endured into later centuries, when entrepreneurial hustlers bottled and sold the elixir in vast quantities, touting it as an effective 'purgative', a convenient catch-all promising to soothe whatever ailed you. Summer crowds gathered on the green at Oak Common to soak in the therapeutic surroundings, enjoy hearty breakfasts in the open air and perhaps play away lazy afternoons at one of Acton's popular outdoor bowling alleys.

As in most popular holiday destinations, Acton's settled population did their best to carry on with their day-to-day lives in spite of the ever-increasing traffic filling the streets and common areas. Acton may have been a popular tourist destination, but it was first and foremost a farming community that was largely composed of tenant farmers who leased land from the wealthy owners of large agricultural holdings. These farmers worked their fields in strips, tended orchards and grazed their livestock of horses, sheep and fat cows upon Acton's rich arable pastures and common grounds. So lush and verdant were Acton's meadows and grazing lands that one local innkeeper remarked that they had never once seen a herd of barren or dry cattle. Fragmentary records from the seventeenth century show that Acton boasted a wealth of supporting businesses and trades, including several mills, a tannery, brick works, blacksmiths, breweries, tailors and weavers to name just a few. The agricultural roots of the community reached back to its ancient past, when Acton was named 'Oak Town' by the

Anglo-Saxons. The traditional cycles of rural life not only endured, but prospered alongside the town's exponential urban growth and the fashionable new craze for healing waters and summer escapes.

There lived within the embrace of Acton's charming estates a woman who was, according to all accounts, the ideal embodiment of genteel femininity. Margret Vincent, thirty-two years old, was the beloved wife of Jarvis Vincent and the devoted mother of three pretty sons: a newborn baby and two boys aged two and five. She was the obedient daughter of a parish churchwarden and had been born and raised as an Anglican in the town of Rickmansworth in Hertfordshire. Margret married Jarvis on 5 November 1606, at the church of St Magnus in London. Shortly afterwards they settled in Acton to raise a family. Her marriage was a happy one, a blessed love match to a gentleman of good standing that afforded her a life of affluent ease and mutual affection. She lived in a fine house that was well furnished and she was well served by a maid of all work and a wet nurse, who eased the burden of feeding and caring for the youngest child. As suited a woman of her station, Margret dressed in the height of early-seventeenth-century fashion. She wore tight-sleeved dresses with long, narrow bodices and intricate, finely lacy standing collars, open-fronted gowns adorned with close-fitted cartwheel ruffs, lace trims, winged sleeves and beautiful headdresses finished with an assortment of fine jewellery. Margret was a well-liked woman in her community and was described by her friends and neighbours as 'well educated', 'discreet', 'civil' and 'of good conversation', comporting herself with the dignity and pride of a woman, a wife and a mother.

Margret lived her life suitably ensconced within the family home, surrounded by her children and attending to the duties of her sex. In the early modern period parenting was split according to rigid gender roles. Men inhabited the public world and freely engaged in business, politics and trade, and were responsible for supporting their families both financially and authoritatively. In the domestic commonwealth the father was the *pater familias*, the master of his domain. If men were the masters then women were their subjects, and their place was in the home. Society held that women were, by nature, nurturing beings whose primary function in life was the rearing of children. Inhabiting the role of an ideal mother was important to women of the middling and upper classes, who viewed motherhood as both a sacred duty and a joy. Family life was their whole life and their female social identity was inseparable from maternity. As a woman belonging to the middle classes, Margret was expected to manage the home and the household servants, care for her sons and oversee their education until the age of seven, when they would begin their transition from the private sphere of childhood into the public world of men. Motherhood suited Margret well, and with the assistance of her maid and wet nurse she embraced her responsibilities and flourished. Her children were a joy to her, and she was not alone in her loving devotion to them: the eldest, Tom, was the especial favourite of Nan the maid, who had known and loved him from the moment he was born.

In her faith Margret was deeply religious, and she often sought the counsel of spiritual advisors to guide her as she endeavoured to be the best wife and mother. In turn it was her duty to instruct her children in their proper moral and religious behaviour, and through the example of her own religious practice she hoped to be a guiding light for them. She had always acted according to what she believed to be in the best interests of her children, and yet it was during her consultations with her religious advisors that things began to change for the worse. At this time Margret had fallen into the subversive company of some Catholic members of her community. By that association she had become exposed to their teachings and before long their 'subtill sophistry' and 'charming perswasions' had led her to question, and then abandon, her Protestant faith. Anti-Catholic propaganda would have it that Margret was a fool who had fallen under a devilish spell; however in reality she was an intelligent, thoughtful and well-read woman whose conversion came about after a great deal of introspection.

Yet her agency in the personal matter of her faith was not to be entertained by a staunchly Protestant majority who held that such desertions should be attributed to the weakness of the female sex; certain women, it was said, were especially vulnerable to the enticements of bad actors.

Over time Margret had become a steadfast Catholic, and as her faith grew stronger so too did her concern for the condition and destination of her family's eternal souls. Encouraged by her spiritual advisors and led by her own conscience, she began to work on her husband Jarvis to turn his back upon what she perceived to be his misguided Protestantism. Only by becoming a Catholic could his soul be saved. This was dangerous talk, for England in the early years of the seventeenth century was not a safe place for Catholics to preach their faith. When James Stuart ascended the throne in 1603 there had been whispers of hope that his reign would result in greater tolerance towards England's Catholic community. Yet this hope was a fragile one, and was barely sustained in the years of hostility that followed the failed Gunpowder Plot of 1605. Protestant clerics produced huge quantities of anti-Catholic propaganda and John Foxe's polemic work of Protestant martyrology, *Acts and Monuments*, was quickly reprinted to satisfy the public's ever-growing appetite for violent stories of Protestant heroes and dastardly Catholic villains. In 1606 the Jacobean Oath of Allegiance was passed into law, demanding that all Catholics swore loyalty to the King of England over their allegiance to the Pope in Rome. Enshrined in statute law was the ever-present fear that Catholics were a scheming lot whose loyalty to king and county was deeply suspect. Failure to swear such an oath could have fatal consequences, as was seen between the years of 1607 and 1618 when a number of Catholic clergymen, having failed to swear the oath, were found guilty of treason and sentenced to death. The majority of moderate English Catholics – those everyday folk who simply wished to practise their individual faith in peace – were caught in the crossfire between a radical Catholic minority and a Protestant majority who would not soon forget or forgive the bloody reign of Queen Mary.

Margret tried in vain to convert her husband to what she believed to be 'the light of true understanding'. This was not simply a matter of faith but a matter of the heart. Margret loved her family and it must have pained her terribly to imagine that, according to her faith, the present courses of their lives would lead them all to damnation. Hers was not a mission to please her religious advisors so much as it was a battle to save the very souls of her beloved family. Yet Jarvis was not to be moved; he was deeply grounded in his own religious beliefs and determined to uphold his position as a good, religious man within his community. It was embarrassing for him to be lectured by his wife, and by his faith and his station as the man of the house he could not tolerate her behaviour. He scorned her attempts to convert him as 'vain and frivolous', and chastised her for being an undutiful wife by shaming her with 'many unkind speeches'. Eventually he put his foot down and forbade Margret to raise their children in the Catholic way. This was a devastating blow for Margret, and from that moment onwards the loving bond between husband and wife was irrevocably damaged. The matter of souls was far too important and could not simply, in the name of domestic harmony, be swept under the rug. The conflict between them was frustratingly unequal, for although Margret was the mistress of house and home, Jarvis was her master, and his word was law.

At every step Margret's efforts to covert her husband were frustrated, and with each passing day she grew more and more desperate. In her mind she was failing her children in the worst possible way, for she believed that unless she was able to raise them within the Catholic faith their souls would be forever lost. Margret could not abandon her children to the fires of hell, 'a place of infinite and extreme torment' according to the minster Thomas Phillips in his frightening treatise *The Book of Lamentations*. That hell existed was not a matter of contention between Catholics and Protestants, and while their strategies for avoiding damnation may have differed, authorities on both sides of the religious divide happily conjured up images of excruciating suffering intended to 'force tears from the eyes of the simple and ignorant'. As a former Protestant and converted Catholic Margret would have been well versed in lurid descriptions of hell: that dread place, a prison of darkness, where fire and brimstone burned eternally upon the tortured bodies of the damned. How she must have quailed at the prospect of her three young sons being condemned to such a fate, and how she must have burst with impotent frustration as her husband repeatedly swept aside her attempts to save her family.

As a married gentlewoman of good standing Margret's status as a wife and mother underpinned not only her social identity but also her individual sense of value. She found herself in an impossible situation in which her choices had been stripped away, her authority undermined, her self-worth diminished and the safety of her children's souls placed in peril. Conventional wisdom held that it would be sheer folly to press a desperate foe too hard, and a mother motivated by despair may be forced to commit reckless, furious acts. In 1610 the gentlewoman Elizabeth Grymestone wrote: 'There is nothing so strong as the force of love; there is no love so forcible as the love of an affectionate mother to her naturall child.' This sentiment was brought to a radical conclusion by Dorothy Leigh in her 1616 work *The Mother's Blessing* when she wrote: 'and will not a Mother venture to offend the world for her children's sake . . . for the love of a mother to her children is hardly contained within the bounds of reason'. Margret had been pushed beyond the threshold of reason. She had no recourse left to her, nowhere to turn and nothing left to lose. Torn between the forces of a mother's love and a woman's duty, she broke, and became determined to do whatever she must to save the souls of her beloved children before the rot of their misguided faith could take hold: she had to kill them.

Margret bided her time, waiting for the perfect opportunity to put her desperate plan into action. It wasn't long before a chance presented itself. During the summer of 1616 there was an ongoing feud between the towns of Acton and Willesden, which each shared a border on an area of hotly contested common land. The citizens of Acton believed that they had the greater right to the land, and so jealously guarded it from Willesden's marauding cattle. Protection of the common was an effort shared by the entire farming community, who had formed a kind of neighbourhood watch to patrol the common and chase away unwelcome livestock. On Thursday, 9 May, after divine service was finished, the women of Acton met in town with the idea that they wanted to help their husbands by taking a turn at defending the common. The gathering of so many formidable women, as righteously indignant as those embroiled in neighbourly disputes liked to be, must have been a vastly amusing sight to the London gentry taking their leisure there. Before the determined body of women set about their duty they first called upon Margret, who had earlier promised to join them. Margret feigned illness and begged to be excused from her promise, offering to send her maid Nan in her stead. The women of Acton gladly accepted this substitute and bid Margret farewell.

At last Margret was alone and had the opportunity to put her murderous plan into action. To her frustration her youngest son was away 'at nurse' in another household; however her two eldest boys were inside the house. It was not ideal as she had hoped to kill all her children in one fell swoop, however she was determined to make do with the circumstances at hand. It was now or never. Reaching under her skirts, she unfastened one of her stocking garters and tied it into a noose. She then locked the doors and went in search of her children. First she went to the youngest of the two boys, who at just two years old could not interpret the look of intent upon his mother's face, nor the meaning of the noose that was gripped so painfully in her hand. Margret seized her son by his throat, slipped the ligature about his head and in a moment of violence wrenched the life out of his small body. After the deed was done she carried him into her bedroom and carefully laid his still-warm body upon her bed. Yet her task was incomplete. Turning on her heel, she strode through the house until she found her five-year-old son playing alone in a quiet corner. Without hesitation she gathered him into her arms and strangled him to death. She bore his small, lifeless form into her bedroom and laid it with tender care next to her other child. There they remained, two little brothers who that morning had been roused from their beds and dressed in fine clothes, who had bickered and laughed and perhaps even been caught up in the excitement of the women's rally to defend the common. Now they lay dead, murdered by hands that only a few hours earlier had caressed them with a mother's love.

In the silence that followed those agonised minutes of violence, Margret became desperate and struggled to kill herself. First she took the garter that had so recently ended the lives of her children and tied it about her own neck in a futile attempt to strangle herself. It was an impossible endeavour and so, abandoning that frantic effort, she ran out of the back door and into the yard with the intention on throwing herself into the pond. At this moment her maid Nan, who for some unknown reason had tuned back from the common, walked into the yard and saw her mistress in a terrible state. Perceiving Margret's haunted expression, Nan guessed that something dreadful had happened and begged to know how the children fared.

'Oh Nan!' Margret wept. 'Never oh never shalt thou see thy Tom again.' At once they fell upon each other, not in mutual grief but in a despairing struggle. Margret beat Nan about the head, but Nan was the stronger of the two and she wrestled her mistress into submission. Nan screamed for aid, and on hearing her cries several neighbours ran to give her assistance. The neighbours were soon followed by Jarvis, who was shocked by the noise and commotion coming from his own backyard. There he saw his once mild and affectionate wife restrained on the floor, red-faced and heaving with grief. Without a word he ran into the house, where he discovered the bodies of his two murdered sons.

In those strange moments just after an unimaginable tragedy, there often follows a hopeless kicking of the heels and wringing of hands as each person attempts to situate themselves in their shocking new reality. Once the children had been discovered, the crowd that had gathered in the yard stood in stunned silence, each of them unwilling actors in some other-worldly play for which they had no script and no direction. Some wept, some stared in amazement and others took off running to summon neighbours, as though fresh eyes upon the scene would generate fresh ideas as to what could be said or done.

At last Jarvis returned to his wife's side and, breaking the dreadful silence, he cried:

'Oh Margret, Margret, how often have I perswaded thee from this damned opinion, this damned opinion that hath undone us all!'

'Oh Jarvis!' Margret shot back. 'This had never beene done if thou hadst been ruld, and by mee converted. But what is done is past, for they are saints in heaven, and I nothing to repent it.'

In such a way they raged back and forth, each utterly convinced that the fault lay with the other. Jarvis believed that his wife had been bewitched by the lies of scheming papists, and Margret was convinced that her husband's obstinacy had forced her hand.

As the news of the killings began to spread, the stunned community reacted with outcries of horror and disbelief. It seemed impossible for the public imagination to situate motherhood and murder side by side. How could a mother be moved to commit such violent acts upon those whom nature dictated she was to love and protect? There could be no satisfactory answer to such a question, and so pamphleteers reporting upon the crime sought to strip Margret of her maternity and re-dress her instead as a monster. The years of Margret's life in which she was a kind woman and devoted mother were erased in but a moment, and all that remained were distorted, bestial shadows. She was described as being 'more cruell than the viper, the invenomd serpent, the snake, or any beast whatsoever, against all kind'. She was a 'tigress', a 'creature not deserving mothers name' and 'more unnatural than pagan, caniball, savage, beast or fowle'. Her crimes were held to have been driven by the pricking lances of malevolent demons. This was a time when emerging concepts of the causes of mental illness were intermixed with superstition and an ever-present fear of devils, demons and witches. As Margret killed her children she was said to have been 'assisted by the devill' and 'bewitched with a witchcraft begot by hell'. A woodcut illustration depicting Margret in the act of pulling a cord tightly round the neck of one of her sons shows a demon with black wings, sagging breasts and clawed feet standing at her side as an accomplice in murder, offering up two more lengths of rope to finish what had been started.

The reactions of the early modern presses to Margret's crimes may strike a familiar chord with modern readers. Our own news media and true-crime publications take pains to emphasise the monstrous aspect of mothers who kill their children. Such women are portrayed as betrayers of their sex, inhuman, crazy, evil, morally corrupt and devoid of feeling. Their crimes evoke a deep sense of outrage. Like the early moderns, it seems impossible for us to acknowledge the humanity and maternity of women who have murdered their children, as though to do so would be to betray their victims. However, failure to reconcile motherhood with murder reduces complex causes and conditions into horror stories where metaphorical monsters and devils walk the earth to wreak havoc upon innocent souls. By dehumanising murderous mothers the true-crime presses of the early modern period sought to delegitimise the dangerous idea that women were capable of acting in opposition to their biological natures – natures which dictated that they must be gentle, nurturing and non-violent caregivers; that, like men, women too were more than capable of committing diabolical acts If one good gentlewoman violently subverted the laws of nature and society, then what did this mean for all of womankind? It was unthinkable to acknowledge the agency of women to act outside their natures; it was far easier for a traumatised public to reject the humanity, femininity and maternity of women such as Margret.

It would not have entered into the minds of the early modern public to question the social, cultural, religious and material factors that gave rise to Margret's crimes, and we can never know what she was thinking or feeling when she planned and committed the murder of her children. There was no evidence to suggest that she was mentally ill or suffering from psychosis at the time of the murders, and none of the surviving accounts mention that she was prone to 'melancholia' or 'lunacy'. At a time when hysteria and madness were acknowledged as motivating factors in cases of maternal filicide, they were not considered or discussed in the surviving records of this case. In 1616 Sir Edward Sherburne wrote a letter to his friend Sir Dudley Charelton in which he described in detail the events surrounding Margret's crimes. He noted in particular that 'shee was free from madnes, so is shee still'. None of the women who spoke to Margret immediately before the murders noted anything different in her demeanour or speech. It was also highly unlikely that Margret was abusive or neglectful, as even her strongest detractors stated that she was a devoted and loving mother to her boys. She was not detached or uninterested in their lives, she had no interest in denying her motherhood, nor did she wish to destroy her children in a bid to free herself from the burden of their care. On the contrary, Margret had embraced motherhood and derived a great deal of joy from her sons.

It is possible that Margret killed her children as an act of vengeance against her husband Jarvis, who had mocked her new-found faith and spurned her desperate efforts to save her family from what she believed to be eternal damnation. Historical records of maternal filicides driven by motives of revenge are extremely rare, but such crimes did happen, as can be seen in a pamphlet from 1690 which tells the tragic story of Katherine Fox of Chatham. Her husband was a violent alcoholic who would viciously beat her when he was taken with drink. So brutal were his attacks that on several occasions Katherine was thought to have been beaten to death. Money that was supposed to be given to Katherine to care for her children was spent on alcohol, and she fell into despair as she watched her two young sons wasting away from hunger. On the fateful day of her crimes Katherine's children were crying to her that they should die from want, while she could only weep in reply, 'Alas! Alas! What shall become of me, or who shall succour you, my children? Better it is to die with one stroke, than to languish in a continual famine.' She at once grasped a knife and without another word slit her children's throats from ear to ear.

After she had cut her sons' throats she sat, still saturated in their blood, and waited for her husband to return. At length he staggered into the kitchen, blind drunk and utterly insensible to the horrific scene laid out before him. He dragged himself into the bedroom and collapsed on to his bed, where he promptly fell asleep. In a fury Katherine snatched up the knife and followed her husband; she leaned over his body and as he slept she cut his throat. Once the deed was done she bitterly admonished his corpse, 'Thou shalt die, thou negligent man, since thy ill government hath been the ruine of me and my children.' These precise words may have been no more than a pamphleteer's flair for the dramatic, and they undermined suggestions that her actions were altruistically motivated. By murdering her sleeping husband Katherine had moved beyond crimes of mercy to a crime of retribution.

Modern studies into cases of maternal filicide show that

mothers who are moved to kill their children are often triggered by a number of social and material stressors in their lives, such as financial troubles, isolation and problems with intimate relationships. These studies also found that the offender may have been emotionally disturbed by the breakdown of the relationship with the father of her children. Of course, we must be careful not to apply like for like the findings of modern studies to historical cultures, yet it is difficult not to be impressed by the comparisons that can be drawn with the case of Margret Vincent. Like the women who commit acts of maternal filicide today, Margret was struggling with similar stressors in her life. Her once-harmonious marriage to Jarvis had descended into one of unrelenting conflict and strife, and her loving husband had become derisive, cold and dismissive upon a matter that meant more to Margret than anything else in her life. She could not be moved from her convictions, and the resulting conflict with her husband only compounded her growing sense of isolation and desperation.

Another common theme in modern cases of maternal filicide is that women harboured fears that their motherhood was under threat. They either felt that they could no longer be the mothers their children needed, or that forces outside their control had robbed them of the ability to care for their children. Margret's valued maternal identity had likewise been completely undermined by her husband's dictates regarding their children's religious education. Where once she had been in charge of her children's moral and religious upbringing, she found herself removed from that role and relegated to the position of a spectator.

For a respectable gentlewoman such as Margret her status as a mother defined both her social and her individual identity. The rigid structures of family life underpinned the very foundations of early modern society, and a citizen's status was firmly grounded in strict hierarchical frameworks. It would have been deeply shameful for Margret to feel as though she had been stripped of the role that defined her worth. Honour was not a virtue reserved just for men; women equally felt the humiliation of public disgrace and strove within the boundaries of their sex to salvage what small measures of dignity they could hold on to. Unable to defy her husband's rule, shamed by her loss of maternal status, overwhelmed by her emotions and driven by a maddening fear that with each passing day her children were tainted with sin, Margret believed she had no option but to kill her sons; not only to save them, but to save her own sense of self.

That Margret's crimes were altruistically motivated is further evidenced by the way she treated her children after she had murdered them. Her actions here too mirror those observed in modern cases of maternal filicide. Margret had removed the garter from round her children's necks before laying them carefully on her bed, as though to arrange them in a sleeping posture. She did not wish to shame or humiliate her children in death, nor did she disregard their bodies. She acted as though they had died by tragic circumstances outside her control, and she tenderly arranged their bodies in the manner of a grieving mother rather than a cold-hearted murderess. It is extremely difficult to understand how a mother can transition from the act of manually strangling her own children to then immediately handling them with such care. Yet this behaviour is often seen in modern cases of maternal filicide, where mothers will bathe and dress the bodies of their children, tuck them into bed and arrange their favourite toys around them. In the minds of those mothers, killing and care are not contradictory actions; they are expressions of a mother's love. Even as Margret murdered her sons she sought to strengthen rather than sever the bonds of maternal affection, for she truly believed that she was committing an act of mercy.

In the immediate aftermath of the killings, as Margret and Jarvis argued in the backyard by the pond, a runner was sent to summon the constable, Mr Dighton. Margret was arrested and taken before Edward Roberts of Willesden, a justice of the peace, who issued a warrant to send her to Newgate Prison in London where she was to remain until her trial at the Court of Sessions. It was late in the day by the time the warrant had been issued, and so it was agreed that Margret would spend the night under arrest at Mr Dighton's house at the Bell in Acton. That night she was surrounded by a strong body of watchmen and neighbours, who not only guarded against her escape but used their time to convince her of the error of her ways. They begged her to acknowledge that she had committed a grievous sin and for the good of her soul they entreated her to repent. However, Margret's 'iron-natured heart' would not be moved. She was reportedly obstinate and proud in her refusal to admit wrongdoing and did not see that she had committed any deed that needed to be forgiven. Nothing could shake her conviction that she had acted in her children's best interests.

On Friday, 10 May Margret was transported to Newgate Prison by Mr Dighton and several of her neighbours. For a gentlewoman accustomed to the finer things in life her relocation to that notoriously cold, dark and frightening place must have been an overwhelming and confusing experience. As Margret was processed at Newgate she was found to be in possession a rosary, a dangerous and reviled object that was quickly taken from her and destroyed. Margret's Catholicism was a serious problem and was perceived to have been the driving force behind her terrible crime. Her friends and family despaired that her continued adherence to what they believed to be a 'dangerous' and 'wicked' faith condemned her soul to an eternity of damnation and could not be tolerated. Over a two-week period Margret was visited by many friends and acquaintances who, through their many 'sweete and comfortable perswasions', sought to convert her back into the fold of the one true faith. They begged Margret to express regret, to say sorry and to admit that she had been in the wrong; however she steadfastly refused, and insisted that 'she had done a deede of charity' by making her sons 'saints in heaven'.

As the trial date loomed Margret's friends became desperate. In the hope that her soul could yet be saved, several preachers were sent for to visit her in Newgate. Margret refused to hear their arguments and would not look upon any Protestant books for fear that it would be dangerous for her to do so. She was so afraid that when she was handed a copy of the Bible in English she threw it across the room, and in a frenzy of 'bewitching wilfulness' turned her head, blocked her ears and refused to listen. Her violent refusal to hear any words contrary to her own faith could be interpreted as a determined effort to uphold her genuine religious beliefs; yet her fear may also have arisen from a dawning suspicion that she had been wrong to kill her children. It suited the vanity of the preachers assigned to her spiritual care to win her over to the Protestant cause. The conversion of such a notorious soul would have been a resounding success in the name of Protestantism, but for Margret their efforts threatened to tear from her a surety of belief that, once lost, could never be recovered. How could she even begin to contemplate the idea that she had killed her precious sons for nothing? After sacrificing so much, how could she accept that her cause was a false one? Outwardly she may have resembled a religious fanatic stubbornly clinging to her faith, but inwardly she was a mother in crisis as she was being forced to concede that she had not been the saviour of her children; she was no more than their murderer.

At last Margret broke. Just a few days before her trial she admitted that she had been in the wrong and that she 'earnestly believed that she had eternally deserved hell fire for the murder of her children'. She repented her deeds, and bitterly cried that if she could go back and have her children alive in her arms again then 'not all the world' could have convinced her to kill them. She gave a full confession and admitted her guilt at trial, and with a 'patient' mind she calmly received her judgment and death sentence. The session roll for her trial is lost, however a brief account from the calendar simply reads: 'Margaret Vincent for the murder of her two sons. Acknowledged to be hanged.' Her execution is also mentioned in Sir Edward Sherburne's letter dated that same year in which he confirms that Margret was duly hanged at Tyburn: 'a just reward for such wickedness'.

It was almost unheard of for married women to be

convicted and executed for the murder of their own children. The hanging of such a rare and notorious murderess would have attracted vast crowds to Tyburn, where both money and elbows would be enthusiastically used in order to secure the best view. Those witnessing Margret's execution must have meditated upon the nature of her crimes to some degree. The dichotomy of female violence had been painfully brought to the forefront of public discourse, and many did not know what to make of Margret Vincent. She was a paradox, a dissonant voice and a puzzle of many parts that refused a satisfactory resolution: the embodiment of idealised femininity and motherhood, and yet a reviled monster capable of unimaginable savagery. Her fragile sex had made her vulnerable to the predatory persuasions of those most hated Roman Catholics, and so while she was viewed as the perpetrator of a terrible crime she was also seen as a victim who had been manipulated by a far greater enemy. Anti-Catholic propagandists thrilled to the fact that her religious beliefs were the motivating force behind her crime, and they could not pass up the opportunity to weave a tale in which wolfish papists poured corruption into the ears of even the most genteel citizens. Nor could they resist glorifying in Margret's repentance while she was imprisoned at Newgate. There she was transformed, washed clean of blood and born again as a God-fearing Protestant. She fitted a narrative of corruption and redemption that made her an ideal character upon whom cautionary tales could be hung.

The tale of Margret's downfall was recounted in the pages of an anti-Catholic true-crime pamphlet titled *A Pittilesse Mother*. Pamphlets such as these were written to shock and offend, and they offer us revealing glimpses into how the early moderns understood and reacted to extreme acts of female violence. This account charted the changing status of Margret from ideal mother to inhuman monster, and then finally penitent victim. She was a woman whose crimes provoked outrage mingled with a kind of incredulous sympathy. Margret's crimes were so incomprehensible that it was not enough for a shell-shocked public to strip her of her femininity and her humanity: they also sought to attribute blame to a greater common enemy – those most hated and reviled 'Romaine wolves', Catholics. It seemed necessary for Margret's crimes to be reframed by a public who were unable to believe that a gentlewoman of good standing could step so dangerously, and so violently, out of line.

The people of Acton reeled with horror as they tried to understand how a woman who had been a pillar of their community could have acted with such murderous violence. Margret had not only killed her children; she had perverted both the sanctified role of motherhood and the laws of nature, and in so doing she had instilled in the public a fear that women had the agency not only to push against the boundaries of their sex but to shatter them through unimaginable acts of violence and cruelty. This could not be tolerated, and so it was far better to attribute the power of subversion to the Catholic enemy, whose cunning words and subtle arguments were ultimately the undoing of an otherwise obedient and worthy woman. Such gruesome narratives of murder lent themselves well to cautionary tales, for it was understood that those who dabbled in subversive acts invited upon themselves tragic outcomes.

THE MUTILATION OF FRANCIS MARSHALL

Situated at the top of a hill, overlooking the lush green landscapes of Essex, sits the ancient village of Good Easter. The village was founded upon a Roman camp named 'Godichestre', and was later settled and expanded by the Anglo-Saxons. By the medieval period, when the local church of St Andrew's was built, the community called their home 'Gods Estre', or God's estate; no wonder, for its elevated situation seemed to have been touched by God's hand. The well-drained lands and ample springs ensured bountiful harvests and the trade routes of old brought wealth to this small yet prosperous farming community. By the seventeenth century agriculture was the heart and soul of Good Easter, and almost all those living in and around the village were employed in that profession. Farms were family concerns, and the community of farming families was close-knit. For hundreds of years generations of the same kin worked side by side, and when unbent from the plough they came together in the village to worship at St Andrew's, or to share gossip over a drink at the local alehouse. One such family were the Marshalls, headed by an elderly yet industrious man named Francis Marshall.

Francis was a wealthy yeoman of Good Easter who held the tenancy of Sowlford Farm, which lay close to the nearby village of High Easter. He was married to a woman named Joan, and between them they were blessed with six children: Samuel, Daniel, Nathaniel, John, Helen and Clementine. Francis was the *pater familias* at the head of a large and respectable family, encompassing not only his impressive brood but also their spouses and a number of grandchildren. At seventy years old Francis occasionally worried that his advanced age was beginning to slow him down; however such concerns would have been surprising to those who knew and loved him best. Francis took a keen and active interest in the management of Sowlford Farm and was often seen mucking in with the workers or putting his hand to the plough. He was by all accounts in good health and was frequently seen going on long walks around the Essex countryside armed with his trusty walking stick. In spirit he was kind, charitable to the poor of his parish and liked by all who knew him. His son Nathaniel described him as a devout and deeply religious man, unfailingly good-natured and 'not apt to offer wronges or injuries to any'.

In March 1619 the Marshall family were beset by tragedy when Samuel, Francis's eldest son, suddenly died. Stunned by that crushing blow of grief, Francis had scarcely drawn breath when the following month his granddaughter Jone likewise passed away. As the head of his family Francis was determined to shield his loved ones from excessive demonstrations of grief and in the months following the deaths of his son and granddaughter he fronted his pain with an outward show of strength. It was a veneer of forced cheerfulness that at times was difficult to maintain. Francis was, after all, a human being and he could not by force of will alone contain the measures of suffering in his heart. In moments of personal crisis his cheerful façade fell away and he lamented to his wife, servants, neighbours and even his landlord 'sundry discontentful speeches'. Francis confessed that he was weary of life and wished to do away with his home, his possessions and the daily troubles they entailed. At times he was weighed down by episodes of deep melancholy and appeared to be greatly 'greived in mind and very much discontented with himself'. His sudden changes of mood did not overmuch concern his family. They initially perceived his changing disposition to be no more than the natural expressions of a father and grandfather in mourning. In their turn Joan and the Marshall children took comfort from Francis's assertions of well-being, and gave sympathy when grief seemed to eclipse all in his mind save for dark and troubling thoughts.

Yet others in the community perceived Francis's moods to be deeply concerning. Given the 'losses and crosses' he had recently endured, several of his acquaintances feared that his grief was too extreme and that he meant to do himself harm. Death in this period was commonplace, but familiarity did not breed unfeeling hearts. 'When grief appears,' wrote Richard Burton a few years later in his popular work *The Anatomy of Melancholy*, 'all other passions vanish.' Then as now people suffered grief deeply, and their distress could be both mentally and physically overwhelming. Melancholy, it was said, 'hinders concoction, refrigerates the heart, takes away stomack, colour and sleep; thickens the blood' and 'contaminates the spirits'. The links between melancholy and suicide were well understood by lay people in the early modern period, and they took seriously the warnings of a friend who hinted – overtly or otherwise – that his future may be uncertain. Francis continued to struggle with his grief, and his lamentations began to weigh heavily upon the consciences of his friends and family.

Several months passed by in this fashion, and by late

June 1619 Francis seemed to have returned to his old self. On Wednesday the 17th and Thursday the 18th of that month he met his son Nathaniel at Sowlford Farm to care for the livestock, weed the corn and plough the fields. Nathaniel remarked that his father was 'in perfect health' and appeared to be 'senceable, industryous and carefull' in his work. Nor did his father seem to be suffering from any obvious 'dispayre or distraction of mynde'. The following day Francis travelled the five miles from his house to the market in Chelmsford, where he purchased the usual day-to-day provisions needed for his household. Friends who saw him in town that day were pleased to report that he was 'free from any trouble' and that he 'went about and intended his ordinary business without manifesting any discontentednes of mynde'. The next day, being Saturday the 20th, Francis was back on his farm and working late. At about six or seven o'clock that evening he went into one of the barns to speak to a farm worker named Thomas Taboe. They chatted about farm business for a while before Francis bid Thomas goodnight. The fine, late evenings of June afforded Francis a pleasant walk over the two miles from Sowlford Farm back to his house in Good Easter. Stick in hand, he set off into the beautiful Essex countryside and was never seen alive again.

As the dark of night fell, Joan became increasingly concerned at her husband's failure to return home. At first she suspected that he had paid an impromptu visit to their son Daniel, who lived some four miles from the Marshall home. Joan dispatched a messenger to call on Daniel, yet he sent word back that had not seen his father that evening. The messenger next went to knock on the doors of friends and neighbours in the hope that Francis could be found with them. Yet again not a soul among them had seen him. Concern soon turned to alarm as Joan feared that her husband may have fallen sick, or that he had been injured on his way home. Perhaps, she imagined, he had tripped and was lying prone in some remote and dark place. With these fears in mind Joan quickly mustered a search party and directed them to expand their efforts beyond the dwelling houses of her neighbours and out into the fields and lanes surrounding Good Easter. The long night drew out, and only by the encroaching light of dawn could a proper search be conducted. The villagers looked in copses, ditches, small ponds and other such places wherein they feared an older man such as Francis may have become lost or injured. They called out his name, and strained their eyes and ears for any sign that he may be nearby. Many in the search party believed he had met with a tragic accident. Yet others recalled Francis's wretched episodes of melancholy and suspected that he had in truth 'made himself away' to commit some dreadful act of violence upon himself.

At around seven o'clock on Sunday morning, in a remote and 'devious melancholy place' one mile outside Good Easter, the body of Francis Marshall was found lying face-down in a shallow pond. His back and the hind part of his head remained above the waterline, while his feet were mired in the filth of a gradually sloped bank. Under one arm lay his usual walking stick, which was still gripped in his hand. Around his body stretched a tangled mass of branches and small boughs that crept over the water from nearby trees and bushes. It was a sad and remote body of water, overgrown and clogged by wilderness and neglect. A cry sounded through the fields to summon the dispersed search party, who quickly gathered to receive the sorry news of the discovery. Nathaniel, who had not been far off at the time, broke through the crowd and stared disbeliev-ingly at the body of his father. How could he even begin to reconcile the sight of that lifeless form with the vital, industrious and generous man he had seen only the day before? And how was he to break the news to his mother, who had recently suffered the loss of her eldest son and granddaughter?

Supported by his friends and neighbours, Nathaniel was forced to set aside his grief and attend to the immediate crisis at hand. He dispatched his servant, Richard Beareman, to hurry at once to the town of Maldon, some twelve miles away, to fetch John Nash, the coroner. It was a sizeable distance to travel, and it took Beareman some time to make the journey. Once he had arrived in Maldon and been admitted into the residence of the coroner, he thoughtlessly blurted out that 'Francis Marshall had drowned himself!' At once Nash flew into action, issuing a warrant for the constable of the hundred to summon a jury and giving strict orders that the body of Francis Marshall must not be moved. At that moment Francis was a suspected *felo de se*, a self-murderer, and both his body and the pond wherein it lay constituted a crime scene. Moving with utmost haste, Nash gathered the accoutrements of his profession and set off at once to Good Easter.

Meanwhile, a large crowd had gathered around the body of Francis Marshall. It was late in the morning, and the Marshall family were growing restless. Several onlookers cried out in dismay that it seemed as if Francis had killed himself, and many feared that once the coroner arrived the grieving Marshall family would be subjected to the harsh punishments inflicted upon the families of suicides. Not only would they be forced to suffer social disgrace and the horrors of profane burial, but they would also be financially ruined by the laws of felony forfeiture. According to law, should Francis's death be ruled a *felo de se* then all he owned would be seized by the king's almoner and handed over to the Crown. Francis's money, goods and chattels would be tallied up and carried out of the family home to be locked away. Nothing would be overlooked, not even a spoon or a spare shirt would be spared. The livestock and equipment from Sowlford Farm would be seized, the lands escheated and all profits surrendered to the king. Joan would be evicted from the family home, and her children would be robbed of their inheritance. Upon a single verdict an entire family could lose everything and be forced into poverty.

The actions of suicides were wholly reviled by the early modern public, however even they baulked at the injustice of laws which sought to punish innocent family members. Many hotly resented a system that imposed cruel hardship upon those who had committed no crime and had done no wrong. Yet some legal writers crowed that those same harsh laws deterred criminal action, for someone contemplating suicide would have to contend with the knowledge that their death would rob their family of everything they owned. Many others supported forfeiture laws for the wholly mercenary reason of financial greed. Unscrupulous officials, from the office of the almoner down, found inventive ways to skim profits from the seized assets of those charged with the crime of self-murder. There was money to be made from suicide.

In the aftermath of a suspected suicide families often scrambled to hide the deceased person's wealth from the grasping hands of the almoner. Samuel Pepys recalled in his dairy an incident when his cousin's husband had attempted suicide and then lay dying in his bed. Before the poor man had succumbed to death his whole family rushed into the house to hide all his movable goods. Pepys himself was sent running 'in great fear' with some valuable flagons clutched in his arms, and the imagined spectre of an enraged almoner hot on his heels. It was common for friends and family immediately to go on the defensive and adopt an 'us or them' attitude in defiance of forfeiture laws. Families of suspected suicides were often tempted to conspire against almoners, either by hiding goods and chattels or by covering up suicides entirely.

As the Marshall family stood by Francis's body they considered the dangerous situation that they found themselves in. Accusations of suicide had been voiced, and the coroner would be arriving at any moment. The newly appointed king's almoner, the Bishop of Lincoln, George Montaigne, would soon be alerted to the situation, whereby he would move with alacrity to lay claim to all of Francis's wealth. It was then two o'clock in the afternoon, and if something were to be done then it must be done at once or else all may be lost. There and then, it was alleged, Joan, the Marshall children and several friends and neighbours put their heads together and hatched a shocking plan – a plan that was driven by grief, desperation and fear. They did not have the time or the resources to hide Francis's goods and chattels from the almoner. Their only hope was to steer the coroner away from any suspicions of suicide by framing Francis's death as a murder. The story they concocted was that of a robbery gone terribly wrong. They had to make it seem as though Francis had been walking alone at night when he was set upon by some roving villain who, having robbed him of his money pouch, had then cruelly beaten him to death before throwing his body into a shallow pond.

Under the pretence of preventing the scene of death from becoming a spectacle, Nathaniel, John and several others pulled Francis's body out of the pond. By that time he had been lying face-down in the water for approximately eighteen hours, and according to witnesses the body had borne signs of this exposure. There was a small hole in the skin next to one eye and another wound on the lower part of one ear, which 'appeared to be but the sucking of some leach or worme in the water'. The body was laid upon the bank, where it was searched for a money bag, which was taken so as to make it appear that Francis had been robbed. Next they heaved Francis's body up and tied it securely to a ladder, brought to the scene to be used as a makeshift stretcher. The body's arms and legs were held fast, but the head lolled through a gap between the rungs. This was apparently done by design, as when the body was transported for over a mile to the Marshall house it was carried in 'a very barbarous and inhuman fashion' with the head of the corpse dragging and scraping across the sun-baked earth. The intention was to injure the head, to gouge and dent it against rocks, thereby giving the impression that Francis had been subjected to a violet beating.

Once the bearers had arrived at the Marshall house it was decided that the damage inflicted upon Francis's body was not severe or convincing enough to fool the coroner. If the family were to succeed then they would have to damage the corpse further. With this purpose in mind they began to mutilate the body of a man they had once dearly loved and admired. Using some unknown implement they viciously beat, slashed and pierced Francis's head, face and neck, causing six or seven distinct 'holes, cuts or wounds'. One witness stated that one of Francis's ears in particular was dreadfully disfigured 'with the bleeding of such hurte', and another said that they saw two large holes in the head that were so severe they could easily have been perceived as death blows. By all accounts the attack was brutal and the injuries inflicted were the product of a great deal of physical violence. The intent was to create an illusion of anonymous savagery, but in truth these wounds had been dealt by the trembling hands of sons, friends and neighbours. This form of abuse was by necessity extremely intimate; there could be no emotional or physical distance from those acts. The perpetrators would have had to have stood close and looked directly into Francis's face. They would have had to feel the impact of every single blow. What bitter outrage the Marshall family must have felt as they believed their hands had been forced by unfair laws and cruel circumstance to brutalise the frail remains of one whose death they had scarcely had time to grieve.

Later that afternoon John Nash arrived in Good Easter. He was chagrined to discover that the body had been moved, and it was on a sour note that he began his inquest. A selection of summoned jurymen presented themselves to the coroner, yet unbeknown to Nash there were among those men several friends and relatives of the Marshall family who had not been included in the initial summons. These men included Richard Luckin, a close friend of Francis; Thomas Tumbridge, who was allegedly married to one of Francis's daughters; and William Field, who was owed money by the Marshall family. All three men had a vested interest in influencing the outcome of the inquest. Concealing their ties to the Marshall family, they approached Nash with the intention of convincing him to swear them on as jurors. Their feigned sincerity and zeal to apply themselves to their civic duty evidently had an effect on the coroner, for he not only swore them on to the jury but he also appointed Luckin as the foreman. This was a significant stroke of good fortune for the Marshall family as they now had their own men on the inside of the inquest to steer the jury's verdict in their favour.

Eighteen jurymen filed into the Marshall home to begin their 'view' of Francis's body. They observed 'dyvers severall hurtes in and about severall partes of his head', and one of the jurors remarked that the corpse appeared to be 'very gaunte and emptie and not att all to be swelled or filled with water as is usuall with personnes drowned'. From the condition of the body the jury quickly inferred that Francis had evidently been cruelly beaten, and that he likely died of these wounds before entering the water since his body did not bear the typical symptoms of drowning. Next the jury were led down to the pond where the body had been discovered that very morning. Here they considered the possibility that Francis had been killed by accident or misadventure. As the jury looked out over the pond they noted that the water was barely a yard deep, and in addition badly overgrown with trees and branches. They agreed that it would have been unlikely that any man should accidentality drown in such a place as he would simply have had to reach out, take hold of some bough and stand up in order to save himself. It also seemed highly unlikely that Francis could have sustained such brutal injuries simply by falling into the low-lying branches. Having ruled out death by drowning, be it by accident or design, the jury could perceive only one likely cause of death: murder.

There was no further need for delay; the jury had seen enough and were ready to present their verdict to the coroner. Nash, however, was not willing to draw the inquest to a close. He believed that the circumstances leading up to Francis's death had to be considered, and so he made the jurors hear the testimonies of material witnesses before reaching their verdict. The jurors duly listened as various friends, servants and neighbours of the Marshall family testified that Francis had been deeply depressed after the death of his son and granddaughter, and that he had said words to the effect that he was tired of life. Some witnesses believed that Francis had anticipated his own death and had attempted to avoid felony forfeiture when he had endeavoured to do away with his house and goods prior to his death. These actions were indeed suspicious, but as far as the jury were concerned they were hardly conclusive. In spite of these testimonies the jury steadfastly maintained that they wanted to return a verdict of death by murder.

By now Nash was becoming frustrated, and more than a little distrustful of his jury. He suspected that several renegade members of the jury were influencing the opinions of the majority. As a coroner he would have been keenly aware of the public's overall hostility towards forfeiture laws, and he knew that families facing destitution could go to desperate measures to cover up a suicide. Something about the case of Francis Marshall did not sit right with Nash. He simply could not accept the jury's verdict, which he angrily declared was 'most false and untue'. At odds with his jury, he ordered the inquest to reconvene at a later date in Colchester.

This break in proceedings allowed time for word of the incident to reach the ears of the king's almoner, George Montaigne. Montaigne was a fiercely ambitious man who had long had designs on the archbishopric of York. He was always looking to press his advantage and to further his position in the Church. By some accounts he was a charming and witty conversationalist who had made a positive impression on the king. He was also lauded as a just and principled man, a stickler for the rules perhaps, but no tyrant. Less reliable sources enjoyed putting about the fiction that he was the son of an itinerant beggar-woman and that as a young boy he had come under the protection of an honourable gentleman while he was on the run from the authorities.

Montaigne's appointment to the office of the king's almoner was by and large an expression of royal patronage, a mark of favour that afforded him some small opportunity to rake in the occasional financial bonus. While it was true that there was money to be made from suicide, in most cases the victim had little of value. A 1504 Nottingham inquest into the suicide of a spinster named Joan Wynspere listed her worldly possessions as simply being a gown, a coat, a vest and small chest. A 1535 inquest into the suicide of Christopher Suger listed his property as a pair of sheets, a blanket, an orange-coloured jacket and a mattress. Such meagre possessions were unlikely to draw much attention; however it was an entirely different matter when the suspected suicide was a wealthy man. Francis Marshall was a far richer prospect and Montaigne was unwilling to let his case go without a fight. While the Marshall family worked to save themselves by convincing the jury to reach a verdict of death by murder, Montaigne hoped to enrich himself by exerting his power over Nash to reach a verdict of death by suicide.

On Thursday, 2 July the coroner's jury were appointed to meet again in Chelmsford. By this time the coroner had had a chance to conduct a more in-depth investigation into the death of Francis Marshall, and he had summoned more witnesses to give evidence pertaining to Francis's diminished mental health. By the design of Montaigne it was ensured that a 'multitude' of evidence was submitted to the inquest: evidence which, it was hoped, would remove all doubt that Francis had indeed killed himself. Yet Montaigne's efforts were to be frustrated as the Marshall family in turn had been interfering behind the scenes. It was alleged by Montaigne that the Marshall family did 'corruptly and unlawfully . . . conceal and deny such material points of evidence' from the inquest, that they had distorted the facts, and even worse exerted 'menaces and threats' upon the jury and witnesses in order to force the verdict in their favour.

One witness caught in the struggle between the Marshall

family and the king's almoner was a woman named Prudence Newell. During her initial examination by Nash she had given evidence under oath stating that she had overheard Francis saying that he wished to 'destroye himself'. Yet she quickly changed her mind and retracted her testimony, even going so far as to deny that she had ever said such a thing. Perhaps she had been menaced by the Marshall family into keeping her silence, or perhaps she had reconsidered where her loyalties lay. Montaigne was furious, yet no matter how hard he pushed this witness she could not be made to comment further. The local community, it seemed, was split: some acted according to their civic duty and came forward to speak to the inquest, while others seemed to resent the intrusion of outsiders and so concealed or retracted their evidence. In response to the threat of forfeiture, many rallied round the Marshall family to offer their protection. It was fortunate for the Marshalls that they were able to rely on an underlying sense of hostility which already existed between local communities and the state.

The jurors were made to review every item of evidence, and Nash urged them to attend carefully to the facts while overtly implying that he would be most unhappy if they continued to put forth their theory of an anonymous murderer in the night. He scolded the jury, stating that by their consciences they knew that Francis Marshall had killed himself, and that any presentment made to the contrary would be a complete lie. The jury remained unmoved and unimpressed by Nash's outrage, and did 'maintayne and avowe . . . that they would give noe other verdict'. They stuck doggedly to their view that Francis had been beaten and murdered by an unknown assailant. Nash in turn refused to accept their verdict. The stalemate could not be broken. By the close of the day a decidedly frazzled Nash had been unable to wring the verdict he wanted from his jury, and so he was once again forced to adjourn the inquest.

On 23 July the inquest was once again rejoined. Nash and Montaigne had used their time to gather even more witnesses and evidence to prove that Francis Marshall had drowned himself. What precisely this evidence was we do not know, however it predictably did not impress itself too much on the jury. Nash remonstrated with the foreman, Luckin, stressing that the jury had not a single shred of evidence to prove that another man had murdered Francis Marshall. Montaigne raged that the jury acted with 'the height of contempt' as they 'persisted in their wicked purpose corruptly and falsely to present that a man unknowne has murthered the said Francys Marshall'. The jurors hotly disagreed, and argued that throughout the inquest they had, first and foremost, been led by their consciences. Upon their view of all the evidence they were in accord as to the right and true verdict: Francis had been 'murthered by a stranger whome they know not'. They were sorry that Nash had difficulty accepting their presentment, however they could not simply change their minds to suit the wishes of an obstinate coroner.

The verdict could no longer be delayed. Nash had no choice but to accept the jury's presentment of death by murder. As was common in cases dealing with an unknown offender, the mysterious killer of Francis Marshall was given the pseudonym 'John Atstyle', a placeholder name similar to our own 'Joe Bloggs'. The jurors found that 'John Atstyle had of his malice forethought given two mortall woundes to the said Fraunces Marshall and so that he the said John Atstyle hadd malitiously and feloniously murthered him'. By this verdict Francis had been acquitted of the charge of *felo de se* and his family were freed from the miseries that would have been forced on them by felony forfeiture. In addition, Francis's body was spared the horrors of profane burial and instead was permitted a Christian interment. At the very least the Marshall family could gain some comfort by laying Francis to rest in consecrated ground. But, in their efforts to save themselves from forfeiture, had they gone too far?

Throughout their ordeal the Marshall family had endured much suffering, but they had also committed terrible deeds. According to Montaigne they were a villainous, violent group of criminals who had been motivated by greed. By his reasoning the crimes of the Marshall family were manifold, unnatural and great. Francis Marshall was a felon who had, as an act of malice, committed the unforgivable crime of self-murder. His family had then tampered with a crime scene, hidden evidence, mutilated a corpse, infiltrated and corrupted his majesty's inquest, threatened witnesses, forged evidence and presented a false verdict. They had defrauded not only the king's almoner, but by proxy the king himself. Montaigne could not accept the verdict reached by the inquest. He was determined to punish the Marshalls for their crimes and force them to relinquish all of their money, goods, chattels and profits. In October Montaigne filed a suit against the Marshall family in the Court of Star Chamber. There he intended to expose their crimes, reverse the findings of the inquest and take from them everything they owned.

The Court of Star Chamber, named for its vividly painted ceiling of stars, was at once a beautiful and terrifying place. The kinds of cases heard in this court were usually public order offences such as riots and assaults, but it also dealt with cases of fraud, forgery and perjury. Freed from the constraints of the common law, the judges in the Court of Star Chamber operated under the power of the king's prerogative. There was no jury in this courtroom; rather the judges acted as the privy council of old, hearing petitions brought before the king and ruling as they saw fit. It was an oppressive and secretive court, and the punishments it meted out were often arbitrary and grievous. Those found guilty were subjected to cruel punishments such as whipping, mutilations, the cutting-off of body parts, branding and pillorying, to name just a few. In theory the Court of Star Chamber was founded on the principles of equity and fair judgment, yet over the years it had become notorious for its overly harsh rulings and sentences. It was a tool of the almoners by which they could undermine the power of the coroner and seize hold of the property of wealthy men accused of suicide. Almoners were positively encouraged to contest the verdicts of coroners' inquests, for they were privileged prosecutors and as such only had to pay half the usual fee to file suit. Montaigne, who was fired equally by fury, ambition and financial necessity, saw no reason why he should not drag the Marshall family into the Court of Star Chamber to answer for their crimes.

In total thirteen people from Good Easter were accused of conspiring to defraud the king's almoner. The leading members of this 'confederate plott' were Joan Marshall and her sons Nathaniel and John, along with the false jurors Richard Luckin, Thomas Tunbridge and William Field. The rest were friends, neighbours and servants of the Marshall family. The bill of complaint submitted by Montaigne to the court included large gaps that he intended to fill with even more names: those of other conspirators whom he had yet to ferret out and expose. The number of people accused in the bill of complaint speaks of the communal nature of their alleged crimes; it seemed as though the leading citizens of Good Easter had pulled together as one to resist forfeiture. Such acts of resistance were not uncommon. Coroners' juries frequently colluded to return false verdicts, and the Court of Star Chamber records overflow with suits against the families of suicides who, in the aftermath of their loss, were accused of conspiring to defraud the almoner. One such case from 1598 concerned John Wilkins, a Norwich grocer, who had committed suicide by slashing his own throat with a knife (a violent method of self-destruction that was alarmingly common in this period). The jury returned a verdict of death by natural causes, and even went so far as to secure the dubious testimonies of a doctor and three surgeons, all of whom stated that John had died from an illness unrelated to the gaping wound in his neck. The judges who sat in the Court of Star Chamber were well aware of such tricks, and looked upon defendants in these cases with suspicious eyes.

The Marshall family were not willing to go down without a fight. They sought the services of a solicitor, and armed with his legal counsel they stepped up to answer each and every one of Montaigne's accusations. They denied that Francis was unduly depressed, and claimed that they did not have 'any cause to feare or suspecte that hee woulde hurte or doe away himself'. On the contrary, they argued that in the weeks leading up to his death Francis had conducted himself in an industrious manner, with enthusiasm for his life and work. Furthermore, they stressed that Francis was a deeply religious man who would not hurt a soul, including his own. As to the matter of Francis attempting to sell or distribute his property prior to his death, these were simply the sensible actions of a man cognisant of his advanced age. He was not attempting to avoid forfeiture, he was merely putting his estate in order. When Francis went missing the Marshall family claimed that they did not imagine that he had gone away to kill himself, and they did not search in lonely, out-of-the-way places with that idea in mind. The Marshall family maintained that Francis had been bludgeoned to death by an unknown killer. They claimed that they had only moved the body because it had been discovered on a Sunday, and so, assuming that the coroner would not deign to work on the Sabbath, they removed it to avoid a spectacle. As to their infiltration of the inquest, this they dismissed as complete fiction. Many of those accused of conspiring to cover up Francis's suicide argued that they had no reason to do so: Thomas Tumbridge denied being married to one of Francis's daughters, and William Field dismissed the debt owned to him by the Marshall family as a paltry £10, an amount that was hardly worth perjuring himself over.

Montaigne had presented a compelling and dramatic story to the Court of Star Chamber, yet the Marshall family had met each of his accusations head-on. Once the bill of complaint and the joint answers of the defendants had been heard, and both sides had been given the opportunity to interrogate the other, the judges were ready to rule on the case. While the records of proceedings for cases heard in the Court of Star Chamber survive, sadly those of judgments have been lost. We cannot know for certain how the judges ruled on this case. We can, however, follow the fate of the Marshall family through other surviving records. Francis Marshall was a wealthy yeoman and in his will he left a sizeable amount of money, along with the tenancy of Sowlford Farm, to his son Nathaniel. When Nathaniel died in 1638 he was able to pass an equally impressive amount of money, as well as the farm tenancy, to his daughters. According to the wills of Francis and Nathaniel Sowlford farm had not been lost, and the Marshall family had remained wealthy. Furthermore, Francis Marshall's burial in 1619 is recorded in the parish of Good Easter, and there is no subsequent record of his body being exhumed, which it would have been if he were later found guilty of being a *felo de se*. It seemed that the Marshall family had won their case in the Court of Star Chamber. They had not only defended themselves against a charge of defrauding the king's almoner, but most importantly they had saved themselves from the misery of forfeiture and profane burial. Meanwhile the furious George Montaigne had been forced to pay his court costs and had withdrawn from the legal fray without a penny.

We can never know what happened to Francis Marshall on that fine June evening in 1619. One side argued that he was murdered, the other that he had drowned himself. There is, perhaps, a third possibility to be considered: that Francis had simply died of natural causes while walking from Sowlford Farm to his house in Good Easter and had fallen into a shallow body of water. This would explain why he was found in the water yet bore no obvious symptoms of death by drowning. For the Marshall family such speculation would have been immaterial, for once the first accusations of suicide had been made they had little choice but to defend themselves against that most ruinous charge. At that moment the Marshalls were responding to a time-critical crisis. They had not only to confront the death of their beloved patriarch, but they also had to deal with the immediate threat of destitution should Francis be found guilty of committing *felo de se*. Having recently suffered so much at the hands of cruel fortune, it is no wonder they seized their chance to save themselves by any means necessary. Yet their response to the threat of forfeiture was extreme, violent and deeply traumatic. Many in the community and beyond must have questioned their methods, yet many others had rallied round to give them their full support.

It was a testament to the Marshall family's popularity within Good Easter that so many of their friends and neighbours had joined together to aid them in their desperate scheme. This support certainly spoke of the close-knit nature of rural communities at the time, but it also revealed the force of hostility that many in those communities felt towards felony forfeiture in cases of suicide. While it is true that the early moderns reviled the actions of suicides, their hostility did not extend to their families. It was common for people to resist the cruel and unjust forfeiture laws by concealing goods and chattels or by covering up suicides; few, however, went so far as to mutilate the corpses of their loved ones. The anger expressed by George Montaigne was not without reason, for he was shocked and appalled by the violence that had been unleashed on the body of Francis Marshall. His suit in the Court of Star Chamber was driven not only by ambition, greed and a dogged attachment to the principles of his office, but also by a moral necessity which demanded that justice must be served.

The Marshall family may have won the day, but at what price? They had moved so quickly, and so violently, to secure their financial futures that they could not have had time to consider the emotional, psychological and spiritual outcomes of their actions. It is one thing to conspire to mislead a jury; it is quite another to drive a weapon into the head of a man who had been so dearly loved and so recently lost. How did one begin to move past such deeds? The burden of grief is a heavy one; it can perhaps be eased by the comfort of financial security, but it can also be made unbearable by the crushing weight of guilt. Censure in this case should not be heaped upon a despairing family in crisis, nor upon the coroner and the almoner, who had acted according to their consciences; rather it was the law itself that was at fault. Felony forfeiture laws were specifically designed to punish the innocent for the alleged crimes of the dead. When Francis died his family had been forced by those unjust laws to make an impossible choice: to be thrown into poverty or to become criminals. They had done no more than choose what they believed to be the lesser of two evils.

THE BLOODY
MIDWIFE OF
POPLAR

It was a calm evening in June 1693 when a mysterious carriage drew through the streets of Poplar in the parish of Stepney, London. As it entered into the finer residential areas it rattled over cobblestones and threw its long shadow over the tidy houses with their charming gabled storeys and red-tiled roofs. The comings and going of this particular carriage excited the curiosity of Poplar's well-to-do citizens, for its single occupant was an unwelcome newcomer to their community. In the latter years of the seventeenth century Poplar was a wealthy commercial hub centred around shipbuilding and maritime trades. The East India Company, the largest commercial employer in London, had settled its shipbuilding yard in the area, where it attracted a great number of supporting industries and workers. Sturdy merchant vessels and grand warships were built on the Thames and the riverside was packed with warehouses, workshops, alehouses and victuallers. Seamen and skilled tradespeople flocked to live and work there, and speculative builders provided a great number of small houses and unconventional terrace rows to accommodate the burgeoning population of East London's riverside communities.

The gentler classes of London were also drawn to the economic success surrounding Poplar. Retired naval officers, knights and gentlemen settled into the more exclusive areas, close to the waterfront yet far enough removed so as not to be disturbed by the hustle and noise of maritime industry. Their houses were of a grander, older sort, built in the previous century by some of London's most fashionable courtiers and leading citizens. By virtue of their occupants' propriety these fine houses seemed to exude a collective air of respectability. Yet a single house among them attracted censorious gossip and dark looks. Its shuttered windows and closed doors deterred neighbourly visitors, and the women who lived within its walls were secretive, strange and deeply suspicious. Under the watchful eyes of neighbours and passing servants the carriage at last drew to a halt in front of that notorious dwelling. A solitary, bent figure aged between fifty and sixty years old alighted from

the carriage and, sparing not a word or look for her neighbours, hurried inside before slamming the front door closed.

The watching neighbours shook their heads at the
diminutive, fierce woman and cast knowing glances among
themselves. The woman's name was Mary Compton, and
she had moved into her large house in Poplar two years
ago with her eighteen-year-old maid and apprentice Mary
St Dunstan. St Dunstan, who was reportedly 'very nosey',
was believed to have been an unwanted bastard whom
Compton had raised from infancy. She liked to gossip with
the neighbouring servants, whom she happily pumped for
information while giving away very little about herself.
Both women jealously guarded their privacy, shunned their
neighbours and were never seen in church. Prior to her
move to Poplar it was rumoured that Compton had lived
in Greenwich and Woolwich, where she had tried her hand
at running both an alehouse and a chandler's shop. While
she may have briefly attempted to make her living in those
few trades open to women, her main profession was that
of midwife. It was said that she had been trained by an
eminent practitioner in London, and that she had been in
the business of delivering babies for over thirty years. She
advertised herself as a midwife for persons of great quality,
and went about her business in a carriage. In addition to
her discreet comings and going, suspicious men had been
seen calling at Compton's house at all hours of the night,

and on occasion she was visited by overseers of the poor, churchwardens and ministers. Stranger still, multiple neighbours had reportedly seen children and babies entering and leaving the property, although how many and how often was uncertain.

Compton was not a conventional midwife, and her overtly secretive nature was truly extraordinary. The early moderns placed great value on neighbourly goodwill, and as a practising midwife she was expected to be a leading, and above all visible, figure in her community. The midwives' principal domain may have been the private sphere of the birthing chamber, however they would be professionally dead if they did not cultivate and maintain wider social connections within their communities. Midwives were judged, above and beyond their ability to safely deliver babies, by their behaviour, friends, marriage, wealth and piety. Midwifery was one of the few licensed professions available to women, and as such they were subjected to a remarkable measure of scrutiny by a society ill at ease with independent working females.

It was important for midwives not only to promote themselves as upstanding members of their parish, but also to distance themselves from lingering stereotypes of midwives as unskilled, grubby, illiterate 'witches' whose intervention in the birthing chamber might do more harm than good. Properly licensed midwives were valued professionals whose gynaecological expertise afforded them a small measure of power usually only afforded to men. They monitored the behaviour and bodies of their female neighbours, they were able to lead investigations into sexual offences and infanticide, and, as we have seen, they were sometimes called upon to act as expert medical witnesses by the coroner and the courts. Their voices were heard, and their actions carried weight. By necessity the midwife was a figure who had to make herself known and available to her neighbours at any hour of the day or night. It was unusual for a professional midwife such as Compton to shun her neighbours; indeed such behaviour should have been career suicide. Yet her secretive conduct seemed to do her no harm; business was booming and she evidently made enough money to set herself up in an area that was usually reserved for 'persons of considerable rank'.

It was assumed, by the comings and goings of parish masters and young children, that Compton had taken on the additional duty of a nurse to unwanted babies, poor infants and orphans. Nursing was a legitimate way for women to earn a living from home by fostering; some nurses were able to command as much as £5 a year per child, the equivalent of about £600 in modern money, and those who were able to take on multiple charges could make a comfortable living. The Poor Relief Act of 1601 had placed the burden of easing poverty squarely on the shoulders of local parishes, and it was the overseers who were tasked with placing babies and young children with nurses. Under the ever-watchful eye of local magistrates, overseers were supposed to make regular enquiries about the children they had fostered out to nurses, ensuring that they were not being subjected to undue cruelty or want. The overseers were also tasked with surveying the poor, as well as setting and collecting a poor tax, known as the parish rate. The monies levied from the parish rate was distributed to those deemed the most deserving in the form of a weekly cash dole, which would have been given directly to the nurses.

Many parishioners resented paying the poor rate and complained bitterly that the overseers spent too much and too freely. Yet the early moderns were not insensitive to the suffering of innocent children. In spite of a general disgust towards the poor, society held that orphans and foundlings were blameless, 'impotent' beings deserving of Christian charity. The impotent poor were set apart from the greater masses of the loathsome poor, those 'rogues, vagabonds and study beggars' who engaged in 'idleness, thefts, whoredomes . . . and almost all kinds of wicked-nesse'. Infants that had been cast by fate into the stews of rank poverty were to be pitied and protected by the parish. They were to be properly raised and educated so that they would not grow to follow their parents, whoever they may have been, into like conditions of criminal depravity. While many vocal members of the community begrudged the provision of the poor dole, they did not wish for it to be abolished completely. The impotent poor must be provided for, so long, they opined, as it was done cheaply.

Compton continued to live beneath a veil of secrecy until just before Whitsun, on or about 5 June 1693. It was late at night, about nine or ten o'clock, when a man named Richard Drake was walking by Compton's house. As he passed her door he heard 'a great noise' from within and, being deeply troubled, he spared not a moment's thought before he rushed inside to see what the matter was. There he saw Compton staggering about the place, insensible with drink and surrounded by children who were pitifully crying with hunger. Drake moved further into the house and peered into a cradle wherein he saw a tiny infant 'tearing, rending and yawning its mouth to and fro for lack of nourishment'. Outraged by this scene of chaotic misery, Drake turned on Compton and demanded to know why she did not give the children 'some victuals'; however she made no answer as she continued to fall about her rooms in a drunken state. Exasperated, Drake took matters into his own hands. He searched the house for food to help the children, but he could find nothing: 'no bread, butter, cheese nor no manner of sustenance whatever'.

How could this be? Surely the overseers provided

Compton with sufficient money to purchase food for her charges? Having discovered nothing but bare cupboards, Drake hastened next door and summoned a neighbour to bring some milk for the baby, who of all the children seemed to be the most in desperate need. After this incident Drake made a complaint to the parish overseers and the churchwardens. If he hoped for them to leap into action, he was to be bitterly disappointed. The overseers did not shift themselves to investigate the condition of Compton's house, nor did they make any enquiries as to the well-being of the children in her care. They did no more than suggest to Compton that she should leave the parish and take her children with her. Out of sight, out of mind, they reasoned. Compton did not thank the parish masters for their warning, nor did she move.

In spite of Drake's report, Compton continued to take in children on behalf of the parish. On 28 February, some seven months after the drunken episode, she took charge of a female infant who was believed to have been around twelve months old. On 14 August a woman named Mary Edwards came to call at Compton's house. Visitors were usually not permitted, however Edwards had once been a child fostered by Compton, and so she was gladly welcomed into the house by her friend the maid St Dunstan. It was not the old midwife and former nurse that Edwards hoped to visit, for she recalled that Compton was a cruel and unkind woman. During her visit Edwards was dismayed to see the dreadful condition of the children in Compton's care. They were ragged, malnourished little things that hid in corners and quietly begged her for sustenance. Edwards cast about the kitchen looking for food, but soon realised there was nothing to be had save for a single piece of cheese.

In an effort to soothe the crying baby she gently picked her up and petted her about the head; however, when she tried to adjust the tiny head-cloth she was horrified to see that it had become fused to the infant's head and ears. Fearing that the baby might be suffering from an infection, Edwards tried to pull the head-cloth away, only to find that in doing so she was peeling the baby's ears off from her head. A neighbour was quickly called for, and between them the women attempted to feed the poor suffering baby with milk and ease her distress by settling her clothes as best as they could around her suppurating wounds.

The situation at Compton's house had become intolerable. On 18 August yet another complaint was made, this time to the minister of the parish. Too much notice had been taken, and action could no longer be deferred. At last the parish sent officials to Compton's house, and three children, including the baby, were rescued. Incredibly, four children were left behind, as presumably the overseers felt that they were hale enough to remain in Compton's care. The baby was rushed to another nurse named Mrs

Greenwood, but there was little hope that she would survive. Greenwood sadly recalled that the baby was already 'in a manner dead' and that she 'stunk most loathsomely'. Her head-cloth was 'perished close to the skull and stuck into the flesh', and 'the ears . . . were as if rotten'. When Greenwood attempted to remove the baby's small clothes it was discovered that the flesh of her buttocks and genitals was festering and falling way, and that she had holes in the skin of her sunken hips. Greenwood did all she could to kindle the weak embers of life in her care, but the baby was too far gone and died three days later.

On Monday, 21 August, immediately after the death of the unnamed baby girl, Greenwood returned to Compton's house only to find that the midwife was out. St Dunstan was at home, and as usual she was surrounded by filth and a cacophony of yells as the four remaining children ran up and down like wild creatures, hiding in 'holes and corners' and crying loudly for food to ease their perishing hunger. St Dunstan stood defiantly by, proud and unashamed by the pitiful misery of her charges. Greenwood, perhaps hoping to get the surviving children away from that dreadful place, approached a young boy of about seven to tell him the baby had died and that he must leave with her with her to help bury it. 'Why,' the boy said, 'there is one child, a brother of mine, lies dead in the cellar. Take them and bury them together.' This pronouncement, delivered with the grim innocence of a child inured to cruelty, sent a shudder of horror through Greenwood. She hastened over to the neighbours to summon aid, and in turn the constable and various parish officials were once again called back to Compton's house. The citizens of Poplar had had enough, and with talk of a body in the cellar it was no longer possible for the parish masters to turn a blind eye to the strange women who lived so secretively in their midst.

Richard Drake, who had not forgotten his earlier confrontation with Compton, was one of the first to arrive on the scene. He had with him George Hurst, an assistant to the churchwarden, Daniel Parnel, the overseer to the poor, and several other masters of the parish. Once they had gathered in Compton's house they began their search and, following the instructions of the young boy, approached the cellar door. Hurst recounted how the door was secured with three bolts, and when they opened it they were greatly disturbed by a 'noisesome smell' from within. The searchers probed every nook and corner of the cellar, before at last Hurst reached up to a shelf to lift down a hand-basket, which he remarked was seemingly full of rags yet very heavy. He carefully drew the rags aside, revealing within the basket the corpses of two small children. They were in a terrible condition, 'as black as a hat' from decay and covered in maggots that 'crawled out of their bodies'. Once uncovered they stunk 'so prodigiously that none could stand it'. With a cry of dismay Hurst fled the cellar to be sick, and was forced to step away from the search so he could steady his nerves with a drink. Drake next looked into the basket and recoiled at the sight. He recalled that the deceased children were 'quite rotten . . . and it could not be discerned whether they were male or female'.

Provoked by his distress, Drake ran from the cellar to confront St Dunstan. His eye fell upon the sad condition of the surviving children and he demanded to know what food she had given them.

'Nothing but cheese,' she said.

'What do you do for drink?'

'Why, I give water.'

'What if you can't get it?' he pressed, referring not just to water but to food and drink in general.

'Then,' St Dunstan haughtily replied, 'we must go without it.'

Drake next questioned her as to the whereabouts of her mistress.

'Why, she is gone to fetch us bread,' she explained.

In fact, Compton had no intention of returning to the house and shortly after this exchange St Dunstan likewise quietly slipped away and made her escape. She did not bother to take any of the children with her, for her attachment to them was as lacking as her capacity for human kindness. Mr Flower, one of the overseers of the poor, took charge of the surviving children. He led them from that house where they had suffered so much and placed them in the charge of other nurses within the parish.

After the discovery of the two small bodies the coroner was called for, and he quickly summoned a jury and empanelled an inquest. Upon hearing the testimonies of those men who had searched the cellar, the coroner suspected that the house may not yet have yielded all of its secrets. Labourers were sent for and were given orders to dig in the cellar. They were directed to concentrate their efforts on patches of soft earth that appeared to have been previously disturbed. Before long they had unearthed the bones and skull fragments of two more children: one set of remains were dry, as though they had been interred under the cellar floor for some time, and the other remains were very fresh, retaining traces of brain matter, blood and hair, as if the victim 'had not been long buried'. Flushed in equals parts by success and trepidation of further horrors to come, the labourers proceeded to turn over every inch of earth in the cellar. As night fell they were bowed with exhausted relief as, thankfully, they had found no more bodies. Yet the search was not over. The coroner ordered the inquest to reconvene the following morning, when he would put the labourers to work excavating the garden.

On Tuesday morning word of the discovery had spread throughout the parish, and as the labourers began to break the earth in Compton's garden they were watched by an increasingly agitated crowd of onlookers. Long-held suspicions against the two strange women were at last vindicated, and the gathered neighbours loudly voiced their outrage and disbelief. Who, they demanded to know, were the parents of these poor children? Some speculated that the deceased were 'by blows', unwanted bastard children that Compton had taken and then cruelly murdered. What woman, they wondered, could be so bloody, so monstrous, so cruel? How could she sleep at night knowing that the wretched bodies of children lay mouldering in her cellar? As the inquest progressed inside the crowds outside became unruly. Some curious spectators sneaked into the house; they picked their way through Compton's rooms and crept into the cellar to steal away some of the children's bones as souvenirs. The stolen remains were reportedly carried to the Ben Johnson's Head, near St Bride's church on Fleet Street, where they were put on display, to the excitement of the alehouse's clientele. As further entertainment the miserable condition of the two babies discovered in the hand-basket was sung about along to the jolly tune of the ballad 'Russell's Farewell'.

The labourers continued to dig, but by the close of Tuesday no more bodies had been discovered. Yet the garden was large and the labourers were nowhere near finished. The coroner decided that his jury could not reach a verdict until the entire garden had been fully excavated, and so the inquest was deferred for a further six days to allow the labourers the time to complete a full search. They continued to dig, and the gossips breathlessly speculated as to what had been found. Rumour had it that six bodies in total had been recovered from Compton's house, and then eight. Some neighbours whispered that they had seen many suspicious hand-baskets, much like the one found in the cellar, being smuggled out of the house. Should each one of those baskets have contained the remnants of some poor unwanted babe, then the total number of Compton's victims may be higher still. When the excavations where completed the following Monday no further bodies had been found. In total there were five victims: the baby who had been rescued and later died, the two infants in the hand-basket, and two infants found under the cellar floor. At last the coroner's inquest was complete, and the verdict held that the cause of death in all cases was felony murder.

It was around this time that Mr Flower had an encounter with a strange woman. Once the bodies had been removed and the hordes of curiosity-seekers driven away, Mr Flower proceeded to shut up Compton's house to secure it against further trespass. Afterwards he returned home, where he was promptly visited by a woman identifying herself as Anne Davies. She first attempted to settle the rent on

Compton's house, before enquiring after the whereabouts of the surviving children. Upon hearing that Mr Flower did not have the children there with him she quickly made her excuses and left without another word. Mr Flower supposed that Davies had hoped to take the children away with her, but the full significance of her visit would not become apparent until later.

Compton and St Dunstan had fled, and word quickly spread throughout the surrounding parishes that the two fugitives were to be apprehended on sight. Those who knew Compton were especially tasked with keeping a watch out for her. On 11 September, at about one o'clock in the afternoon, a woman named Joanne Smith was making her way to The Strand when she spotted Compton and St Dunstan. Joanne was a neighbour of Compton and had been one of the first on the scene to view the blackened corpses in the hand-basket. Seeing the pair now walking so boldly in The Strand lit a fire of indignation within Joanne, and with reckless bravery she called out to St Dunstan:

'How now Mall, where are you awalking? And your mistress?'

'A little way,' St Dunstan replied and, thinking Joanne a friend, she allowed her to draw closer.

Joanne did not hesitate and, rushing forward, cried:

'Aye! You must go no farther; for the children are starved; and there are two found in a hand-basket in the cellar, and they are rotten. And therefore, you must both go along with me!'

At first St Dunstan crossly denied the accusation, but she quickly perceived that Joanne would not be fooled. Exhortation fell to violence and St Dunstan fought desperately with Joanne while Compton stuck at the edges of the fracas with her own frail resistance. Joanne, alarmed and outnumbered, feared she was to be overwhelmed; however, she was soon aided by her fellow citizens, who waded into the fray to help capture the two wanted criminals.

Followed by a roaring crowd and flanked on each side by constables and beadles, Compton and St Dunstan were roughly marched to the Petty Sessions Court in Bloomsbury. Compton had been observed to have carried herself 'with a great deal of confidence, not seeming the least concern'd'. Once they arrived at the courthouse they were examined by several justices of the peace, who also noted Compton's continued contemptuous manner. Affidavits were taken in which Compton and St Dunstan insisted their innocence, before the justices issued warrants committing both of them to Newgate to await trial. When she was first locked up within that most dreadful prison Compton had continued to behave 'very impudently', but as the days passed her act of bravado fell away and soon she became sullen and withdrawn. The chaplain of Newgate visited her on several occasions with the intention of offering her counsel and 'to call to mind the evil course of her life', yet still she would not confess her crimes. Over the next few days Compton's health rapidly declined, and she succumbed to a mysterious illness which had left her unable to walk. It was rumoured that she had tried and failed to commit suicide by imbibing a poison that ravaged her body, 'as a French midwife of Paris did on like occasions some years since'.

Compton and St Dunstan's trial was scheduled at the Old Bailey on or about 13 September. For over three centuries the Old Bailey has been the locus for some of the most serious and infamous criminal trials in English legal history. Its huge grey walls loom over the street for which it was named, and within its imposing courtrooms the fates of men, women and children have been weighed upon the scales of justice. The original courthouse was destroyed in the Great Fire of London in 1666, and it was eventually rebuilt in 1673. At the far end of the central ground-floor courtroom the judge presided over all from the bench, where he looked down upon the accused in the dock. The jurors were not seated together in a single group but were arranged in rows on both sides of the courtroom, while high-ranking spectators and various court officials sat above them in balconies. To combat typhus one side of the courtroom was open to the outside. This unusual architectural feature allowed fresh air to sweep away the miasma of disease that clung to the prisoners in the dock, and as an added bonus it granted a grand view of criminal trials to the spectators gathered in the yard outside. Such crowds thrilled to the drama of criminal proceedings and their tempers and emotions frequently ran high. During trials of particular notoriety juries often found themselves swayed, or indeed oppressed, by the ever-present mood of the mob.

Compton's day of judgment had at last arrived; however she had not fully recovered from her illness and was confined to her sickbed. Not to be deterred by this complication, her jailers simply tied her to a chair before ignominiously hauling her on to a porter's back to be carried the short distance from Newgate to the Old Bailey. It was unlikely that she made the journey unmolested or unmoved by the hostility of the masses who had gathered to see the infamous 'bloody midwife of Poplar' in the flesh. Was she as monstrous as they had imagined? Did she compare to the hideous likeness of her that was printed in the popular broadside ballads: a haggard, hook-nosed witch with the devil's eyes and grasping claws? No doubt the jeering crowds were at once gratified and disappointed to see that she was not a fiend but simply a diminished woman strapped to a chair. Those who had secured prime positions in the spectators' courtyard that day were to be bitterly disappointed, for when the judge set eyes upon Compton's pitiful condition he declared that she was too ill to stand trail. The trial was postponed to the next sessions, which were not until October. Still bound to her chair, Compton was once more hoisted on to the back of the weary porter to be bumped, jostled and harassed through the streets and back to the freezing confines of her jail cell.

The trial, which was to be presided over by Lord Chief Justice Holt, was set to begin on Thursday, 19 October, at about ten o'clock in the morning. Compton, still 'being very lame in her limbs', was once more bound to a chair and carried through the hostile crowds of London to the courthouse. St Dunstan, who was to stand trial at the same time, stood beside her mistress in the dock. The atmosphere was electric and Justice Holt was forced to calm the hum of murmured excitement before signalling the clerk to proceed. The clerk turned to the accused and bid them raise their hands, before reading out the indictments upon which they were charged. Compton was charged with 'feloniously, wilfully, maliciously and devilishly ... [committing] felony and murder', and St Dunstan with 'abetting, aiding and assisting' in those crimes. Although the trial record confirms that there had been five victims in total, Compton was only indicted on four counts of murder. Her victims were the unnamed female infant, an unnamed male child, a male child named John and a female infant named Anne.

'How say you,' the clerk continued, 'are you guilty of this felony and murder whereof you stand indicted, or not guilty?'

'Not guilty,' they replied in turn.

The indictments having been read and answered, the prisoners were sent back to Newgate to await the trial proper, which was to be held the following day on Friday, 20 October. Justice Holt, perceiving that Compton was very frail and hard of hearing, leaned down in his seat to instruct her to pay attention and listen well to the evidence given against her, for she was on trial for her life. The king's coroner called the evidence, and over the course of the trial fifteen witnesses were summoned to testify against the accused. Richard Drake was the first to be called. He described to the court in distressing detail his previous encounters with Compton, her disreputable behaviour and drunkenness and the poor baby with the rotted flesh. He recounted the horror of finding the badly decomposed bodies of children in Compton's cellar, and the defiant St Dunstan who had scorned his censure. Once Drake had finished giving his evidence he remained at the stand as Justice Holt turned to address the accused.

'Old woman,' he said, directing her attention to Drake, 'will you ask this man any questions?'

She had none, but instead cried out: 'He is the greatest rogue in England! A wicked liar!'

This outburst did not impress the jury, although no doubt it delighted the attending crowds who were closely watching proceedings through the open wall of the courtroom. After

Drake had been dismissed there followed repeated testimonies confirming his version of events. One after another public officials, nurses, churchwardens, overseers of the poor and reputable citizens of Poplar each took the stand to catalogue every inch of suffering that Compton had wrought upon her victims. Throughout these testimonies Compton bristled indignantly, and with each witness in turn her pretence of fragility was replaced by furious defiance.

During these testimonies the plans of a strange woman named Anne Davies were at last brought to light. She was a neighbour of Compton's, and if not a friend then certainly an accomplice. It was revealed that Davies had harboured the fugitives after they had fled, and she further conspired to aid them by attempting to cover up their crimes. On the day that she visited Mr Flower with the excuse of settling the rent on Compton's house, she in truth hoped to take the surviving children away with her. What exactly she planned to do with them afterwards was not openly speculated upon in court, but members of the jury drew their own terrible inferences. The young boy who had revealed the location of the bodies had already said too much, and it would have been of benefit to Compton and St Dunstan to have him and the other children silenced. Compton, anticipating that the game was soon to be up, had further instructed Davies to hurry to her house to dig up the bodies in the cellar, bear them away and hide them as best she could. To Compton's dismay, Davies had arrived too late and had been forced to abandon her scheme. Another witness claimed that Davies had previously taken a dead child from the house and buried it in secret. 'It plainly appeared', the court record reads, '. . . that she was an accessory to the old midwife.'

Had the surviving children been old enough to testify, their evidence would have been the most damning of all. By law their voices could not have been heard in court; however that did not stop the true-crime presses from reporting, and dramatically enlarging upon, the various statements made by the seven-year-old boy whose brother was one of the victims. In one account the boy assumed a far more dramatic role. It was said that he had been left alone the entire day to care for the starving baby girl until he could no longer endure the sound of her pitiful cries. Clutching her in his arms, he moved to a front-facing window and shouted into the street for aid. The son of a neighbour happened to be passing by and, hearing the boy's call, he rushed over to see what was the matter. The boy confided that he had been left alone and was at a loss, for he had no food or drink to ease their hunger. Together the two boys took the baby and walked into the street to rouse the neighbours. Once the constables and parish officials had finally arrived the young boy led them into the house, revealing to them the macabre secrets that lay behind the thrice-bolted cellar door. It was a touching fiction in which a once-powerless victim had thrown open the windows to that awful house and shed light upon his suffering. At last it could be acknowledged and avenged.

At length the prosecution for the Crown rested their case and Compton was given the opportunity to defend herself. Justice Holt turned to address her.

'You are charged with the murder of several children,' he said, 'by starving them to death. There were two children found upon a shelf, and the very vermine crawled about them; Why did you not bury them at the usual place? Why did you conceal them? There was two pieces of skull found in the cellar; one seemed to be fresh, and had the brains; the other was putrified.'

'My Lord!', Compton rudely interjected, 'I did not bury them there.'

'Why did you not give account what became of those children? Why did you go away and leave your house?' he asked.

'Why because I was forced to it, for fear of being arrested!' she cried, as though she was the injured party in the whole dreadful affair. 'I dust not come at my house; I was arrested but a little before, and the children taken with a looseness and vomiting. And because I was not at home, my maid could not bury them.'

Compton claimed she had been persecuted by Richard Drake, who had threatened to arrest her over an unrelated legal matter concerning some money she owed to a certain Mr Stone.

'This man Drake', she ranted, 'is a great rogue!'

She said that Drake's threats to place her under arrest had forced her to run away, and it was during her absence that the children under her care had succumbed to a sudden and severe bout of vomiting and diarrhoea. The fault, Compton complained, was not her own but Drake's. Had she been at home, had she been left alone to do her job and care for her children, then none of this would have happened.

Drake coolly held his tongue, and the court likewise sat in postures of stiff reserve as Compton called character witnesses to testify on her behalf. These witnesses, six in total, confirmed that they had known Compton for several years, and during that time they believed her to have been a woman of good character. None of them were willing to speak on her behalf concerning the matter of the murdered children. It was a painfully weak defence, and sensing that her character witnesses had failed to move the jury, Compton returned to her previous tactic of blaming Drake.

'My Lord!', she burst out, 'my children never wanted for anything, tho I was not at home.' She continued to argue that Drake's threats had driven her from her house, thus depriving the children of her care when they unexpectedly fell ill. 'This fellow Drake has arrested me . . . and I was fain to keep abroad.'

'Prove that any body occasioned you to be absent from your house,' Justice Holt demanded.

'I never arrested her in my life,' Drake interceded, 'but I told her there was an action would come out against her, that was all.'

'You're a lying rogue!'

Compton's anger exploded, causing Justice Holt to issue her a warning that she should watch her tongue and hold her temper in check. Under such circumstances, he advised her, it would be prudent to present herself calmly, and to make the best defence she could. Yet the damage was done; it was plain for all to see that Compton's foul humours ran hot and that the only remorse she felt was for herself. After issuing his admonition Justice Holt asked if she had anything further to say. 'No My Lord,' she replied, drawing to a close her disastrous defence.

St Dunstan was able to stage a far more effective defence. She told the court that Compton had up and vanished for a whole six weeks, leaving her (a mere servant) with no word, no money and no food. In the circumstances she did as best as she could. She swore that she was unaware of the corpses that lay hidden in the cellar, and was as amazed as the rest when their grim discovery was made. The court agreed that there was very little evidence against St Dunstan, and so instead of remonstrating with her they instead began to ponder the question as to how and why so many vulnerable children had been left to perish in Compton's hands. Where were the overseers of the poor throughout all of this? What of the churchwardens who had been seen visiting Compton's house over the last two years? Were they all of them unaware of the rank conditions of the house, the stench of decay, the state of the ragged children huddled in corners or the pitiful babies in their cots who cried for sustenance? Compton's victims were supposed to be protégés of the parish. It was the legal duty of the overseers and the church-wardens to care for those children, to ensure they were well raised and that they came to no harm. Justice Holt turned his furious attention upon the parish masters and demanded to know how it was possible for children in their care to have been starved to death.

Justice Holt made clear his disdain for the parish officials, and all in attendance in the courtroom knew of the reputation of the overseers, whose primary concerns were economic rather than philanthropic. It was said that the overseers cared more for the money in their purses than they did for the lives of their unwanted bastards, foundlings and orphans. Overseers were unpopular figures who attracted a great deal of public hostility. It was an appointed position reluctantly taken on by yeomen, husbandmen and skilled craftsmen of the parish, who did their duty not because they wanted to but because they had to. They were overworked, unpaid and greatly inconvenienced by the burdens of the poor. At all times the overseers were subject to intense scrutiny by a public who resented paying the poor rates and exerted constant pressure on them to curb spending. Unwanted babies were a drain on the public purse and overseers were always on the lookout for ways in which they could cut corners. Respectable nurses commanded a yearly payment to raise unwanted children, so when Compton approached the parish masters with an offer to take those children for a one-off payment of £3 to £5 they were quick to agree. Compton would not only take the children off of their hands, she would also take them off their books. As one pamphleteer wrote: 'for all the ends and designs of church wardens and overseers now-adays was to secure their parishes, and had but little respect to the life and well-being of the infants'.

Nobody cared to ask Compton what she did with the children; indeed it suited the parish masters as much as it did Compton to simply let them perish. Each poor life snuffed out in the cradle represented a great deal of future savings for the parish, and each small corpse spirited away in a hand-basket was freed space for another cash payment. In later centuries, commercially-run operations in which the lives of infants were turned over for the saving and profit of their dole fee arrangements came to be known as 'baby farms'. Such horrors were the *cause célèbre* of the Victorian age, evoking heartfelt calls for legal and social reform. Charles Dickens's famous literary orphan, Oliver Twist, lived his first years in a baby farm, where he 'rolled about the floor all day' in desperate want while the corrupt nurse in charge pocketed the money intended for his care. Censure for such practices was not limited to the nineteenth century; at Compton's trial in 1693 Justice Holt turned his fury on the overseers and churchwardens. The court recorder gleefully recounted that Justice Holt 'did not spare to tell them who are masters of parishes; that by such discreet actions as these, they made themselves accessories to the murder of such poor children in selling their lives for 5.*l* and 3.*l* a child'.

Both the prosecution and defence had been staged, and at last the evidence was summed up. Justice Holt instructed the jury to give their full attention to the 'weighty case' that lay before them, desiring each man to 'be careful, and consider what a most horrid fact the prisoner stood charged with'. The jurors withdrew, and within half an hour returned their verdicts. Mary Compton was found guilty on all four counts of murder and was sentenced to death by hanging. Mary St Dunstan was acquitted due to lack of evidence and Anne Davies was found guilty of accessory to murder and as punishment she was burned in the hand with a branding iron. Compton was promptly rushed out of the courtroom and returned to Newgate to await her execution, which had been set for 22 October.

On the night before her execution Compton was visited by the chaplain of Newgate. He enquired after the condition of her soul and asked whether she was ready to submit herself to God's judgement. With a voice soft and trembling with fear, she continued to deny any wrongdoing and claimed that she had made her peace with God. Those who stood nearby scoffed at her presumption. They believed that an unrepentant murderess such as she was destined to burn in the darkest corner of hell. Later that night Compton dreamed that an angel had visited her in her cell to offer comfort and to reassure her that her soul would be saved. This vision gave her peace of mind and lifted her spirits as she rolled out of bed and readied herself for the gallows. The chaplain, caring not to offer Compton any kindness during her final hours, suggested that the angel was no more than Satan, that 'great enemy of mankind', who disguised himself to trick her and further sink his claws into her damned soul.

With those seeds of doubt cruelly planted in her mind, Compton was heaved into a cart and drawn through the thronged streets from Newgate, along Fleet Street and up Chancery Lane to Holborn, where a great gibbet had been erected. This circuitous route exposed her to a greater number of London's citizens who had turned out en masse to witness her final moments. Once she had arrived at the place of execution she was lifted out of the cart and painfully forced by slow degrees to climb the ladder to the gallows. Witnesses recall that she 'demeaned herself very stubbornly' by rejecting the chaplain's final exhortations, and that even at the very end she refused to seek God's forgiveness. She claimed she did not fear death, 'and at her last breath denied the fact' that she had done any wrong. As the chaplain prayed for her soul she looked away, unaffected and uninterested. With no more to be said or done, the executioner pushed her off the ladder and 'left her to the mercy of Almighty God'.

It was unknown how many victims Mary Compton had murdered during the thirty years she worked as a midwife and nurse. The true-crime presses speculated that Compton had long used her position as a midwife to seek out victims and to negotiate payments from their desperate parents and guardians. Anne Davies claimed that Compton had buried the remains of several unwanted babies in addition to those found in her house. One witness claimed to have seen Compton haunting almshouses and foundling hospitals, where she hoped to relieve the masters of their unwanted burdens and a little coin. The proprietors of such charitable institutions, much like the parish officials of Poplar, may have been more than happy to offload infants that, upon the books and balance sheets, were no more than deficits to be quietly got rid of. Such transactions eased the stresses of the overseers and pleased the rate payers, who inferred that the reduced numbers of impotent poor on the streets could only be a good thing.

In June 1693 the overseers of the poor in the parish of Poplar had been forced to stand on the threshold of a rancid, dark cellar to confront the outcome of their mercenary penny-pinching. Mary Compton had been a cruel and unrepentant murderer, but she would not have been able to run her dreadful operation without the support of the parish masters. For years Compton's neighbours had voiced their concerns, and on more than one occasion the alarm had been officially sounded. Yet the overseers did nothing. They did not wish to know the fates of the children they had sold, or if they did know they did not care. Justice Holt had condemned the overseers as accessories to murder, but they did not suffer any further punishment beyond a public dressing-down. Thankfully, not all of Poplar's leading citizens were content to turn a blind eye to the suffering in their midst. Richard Drake had struggled to make his voice heard, and his evidence at trial was by the far the most detailed and the most damning. But he should not have had to fight for so long and so hard to make his voice heard. His success in court must have been cold comfort indeed, for justice had come too late to save the lives of the five innocent children who had been abandoned to die in the clutches of the bloody midwife of Poplar.

MURDER IN THE
LOLLARDS' TOWER

In December 1514 England rested in the calm before the
storm of the Protestant Reformation. King Henry VIII was
a young yet formidable man of twenty-three who had been
on the throne for five years. His marriage to Catherine of
Aragon was strong; he loved his Spanish-born queen and
hoped that she would give him the son and heir he desperately longed for. The divisive figure of Anne Boleyn was
not to arrive in court for another seven years. The king
was a devout Catholic, England was firmly tied to Rome
and its religious customs were rooted in centuries-old tradi-
tions of medieval Christendom. Sermons were preached
in Latin and priests were the sole mediators between the
common people and the word of God. Prelates of the

Church enjoyed the privilege afforded to them by Papal authority, and they perceived no immediate threat to challenge their power. And why should they? The events that lit the fire keg of religious revolution throughout Europe had not yet occurred: Martin Luther would not post his Ninety-five Theses on the door of a church in Wittenberg until 1517, Thomas Tyndale's translation of the English Bible did not hit the printing presses until 1526, and at this time the king had no intention of divorcing his wife.

These were years of relative peace throughout England. Yet even in these pre-Reformation times there were some who resisted the rule of Catholic orthodoxy by subscribing to the teachings of the medieval theologian John Wycliffe. Their heretical beliefs were broad, but generally held that Scripture should be written in English and made available to all, not just the privileged few who could read Latin. Faith was a matter between the individual and God and was not to be facilitated by the worship of saints or idols; bread was no more than bread, wine was no more than wine, and the ornaments of religious ceremony were no more than material trifles. The people who adhered to these beliefs were derisively labelled 'Lollards', in reference to the wagging of their tongues as they read Scripture to themselves. The very idea of lay men and women reading the Bible was at once laughable and deeply concerning, and was certainly not tolerated by the Church. Lollardy was by necessity practised covertly, for those caught dabbling in unorthodox religious activity were forced to perform humiliating rituals of penance, or at worst they were burned alive at the stake. Lollardy was not a single, cohesive movement but was more a private expression of individual belief, and the Church ruthlessly sought to eradicate even the smallest traces of this religious dissent.

It was put about that Lollards were deranged radicals, but in truth they were everyday men and women; men like Richard Hunne. Richard was a successful and wealthy merchant tailor from the parish of St Margaret in London. He was a man of such good standing in the community that even his enemies described him as a 'very honest person and of good substance'. He may have been an upstanding citizen, but he trod a dangerous line as he made no secret of his disdain for religious authority, and it wasn't long before his behaviour landed him in serious trouble with the Church. In March 1511 Richard's five-week-old son Stephen tragically died while 'at nurse' in the parish of St Mary Matfelon in Whitechapel. The rector of the parish, following ancient custom, demanded that Richard surrender his son's christening gown as payment for the mortuary fee. As a grieving father and a man already harbouring anticlerical sentiments, Richard refused to part with so precious a keepsake. His refusal caused a stir, but it seemed the rector was willing to let the matter lie. Then, just over a year later in April 1512, the same rector cited his complaint on the matter to one of the most powerful ecclesiastical courts in the country: the Archbishop of Canterbury's Court of Audience at Lambeth Palace. This was an extraordinary escalation of legal hostilities, far in excess of what the offence over the christening gown warranted and seemingly out of the blue. Yet Richard was a suspected Lollard, and he had long been a thorn in the side of the Church authorities. They seemed to have had enough of his antics and wanted to deal with him out in the open.

Richard, however, was not the sort of man to meekly fold when presented with the threat of legal action. He made his displeasure widely known, and he argued his case passionately and publicly. This came to a head in December 1512 when his enemy, the rector of St Mary Matfelon, forcibly turfed Richard out of an evensong service while loudly accusing him, to the amazement of the assembled parishioners, of being excommunicate. This was a most outrageous lie and Richard fumed that these false accusations might damage his reputation in the local business community. He furiously met these heavy-handed tactics like for like, and in 1513 he sued the rector for slander and at the same time challenged the legal jurisdiction of the Church in the matter of his son's christening gown by bringing an action of *praemunire*. By now the matter was more than a squabble over a christening gown. Why, Richard demanded to know, should the foreign Papal courts have jurisdiction over English subjects? This was extremely dangerous talk, and in bringing his case Richard had marked himself as enemy of the Church.

In October 1514 the Church at last made its move against Richard. They conducted a raid on his home and seized several illegal items, including books and other works by the Lollard heretic Wycliffe. Richard was arrested for heresy and imprisoned in the Lollards' Tower at St Paul's. On Saturday, 2 December Richard was chained about the neck and taken to Fulham to be examined on five charges of heresy by the Lord Bishop of London, Richard FitzJames. Richard's response to interrogation was at once deferential and defensive; he conceded that some of his words and actions may have unintentionally been heretical in nature, but he carefully avoided any overt admissions of guilt. He would not admit to the charges made against him, and he would not divulge the names of his Lollard friends. In truth Richard believed he had little to fear; the charges against him were flimsy and he countered them with a boastful, arrogant air which infuriated Bishop FitzJames. The interrogation was a flop, and FitzJames had no choice but to return Richard to his cell in the Lollards' Tower. On the morning of Monday, 4 December, less than forty-eight hours after the failed interrogation at Fulham, Richard was found dead, hanged in his cell from a girdle of silk.

When the news of Richard's death reached Bishop FitzJames in Fulham he was quick to accuse Richard of committing the felony offence of *felo de se*, self-murder or suicide. FitzJames saw an opportunity to destroy the good name of a most troublesome enemy, and moved at once to secure Richard's body before the coroner could be summoned. He did not want any interference from the secular arm of the law. Richard had been arrested for religious crimes and had been incarcerated inside the bishop's prison: this was Church business. FitzJames was determined that the coroner of the City of London must not set foot within Richard's prison cell.

On the surface this may have been no more than the jurisdictional posturing of a powerful man intent on exercising his authority over the corpse of a suspected heretic. However, this sort of interference was almost unheard of. When the Lord Mayor of London heard the news of Richard's death he smelled a rat, and immediately dispatched his coroner, Thomas Barnwell, to the Lollards' Tower. Thomas moved with impressive haste and had successfully secured both the body and crime scene before FitzJames, all the way out in Fulham, was able to act. On his arrival at the Lollards' Tower Thomas began his inquest into Richard's death. He summoned twenty-four jurymen from the surrounding parishes and instructed them on their duty: they were expected to examine the body and the crime scene, interview witnesses and potential suspects, deliberate upon all the evidence and then deliver their verdict on the cause of death. The coroner would lead the inquest, but ultimately the verdict was down to the jury. Their duties made clear, the jury were sworn in and led up the narrow spiral staircase and into Richard's cell.

Standing in the doorway of Richard's cell, Thomas and his jurymen viewed the scene before them. The freezing-cold cell was simply furnished and lit by the gloomy light from a single, small-barred window. The jurors glanced at the bed pushed against the far wall and then fixed their eyes on the frightening assortment of stocks, hooks and chains that filled most of the room. There was no mistaking the purpose of this dreadful place: it was a bishop's prison in which suspected heretics and enemies of the Church were put to torture. Richard's body was hanging facing the wall of the cell, suspended from a girdle of black silk tied round his neck, which was secured at the other end to a hook driven into a piece of timber on the wall. Upon first view it would indeed appear as though the desperate prisoner had killed himself, and this conclusion would align with Thomas's professional experience: most non-judicial hangings were suicides. It was an expected formality for a coroner's inquest to rule a hanging in prison as *felo de se*. Yet Thomas was not convinced. Perhaps it was no more than a hunch, or perhaps he was pushing back against the Church's attempt to interfere in his business. Whatever his reason may have been, he was not content to dismiss Richard's death as self-murder. He was determined to do his duty and conduct a thorough investigation.

Copies of Thomas's inquest report survive, and they show that he conducted his investigation with a remarkable awareness of scene preservation and forensic pathology. This is especially impressive considering that sixteenth-century coroners were not medical men; they did not have any formal training and there were no written manuals to guide them in their profession. Thomas instead relied upon his years of vocational experience, coupled with intuition and a familiarity with death that was commonplace to any man or woman living in early modern society. The coroner and his jurymen would have witnessed public hangings, and by first-hand experience would have had expectations as to the condition of a hanging body. This knowledge was crucial to their investigation, as it allowed them to identify the absence of symptoms most commonly associated with asphyxial hanging. Thomas was also aware that by preserving the scene in its original state he might uncover vital evidence that could otherwise be damaged or lost by simply charging in and heaving the body down. So the first part of the inquest was conducted in a 'hands-off' fashion, beginning with a visual examination of the body.

In his inquest report Thomas described Richard's head and face as having a 'fair countenance', meaning he had a clear complexion. This was significant, as victims of hanging would typically be expected to have a blueish hue to their face, which is caused by congestion and the concentration of deoxygenated blood in the head. Another less common yet expected symptom of violent asphyxial death is a characteristic pinprick rash, particularly round the eyes, due to ruptured capillaries. It struck Thomas as strange that Richard not only had none of these symptoms, but his face was remarkably unblemished and free from discolouration. Thomas also noted other suspicious aspects of Richard's appearance: he seemed to have no outward signs of dishevelment around his head or face, his hair was neatly combed and his hat carefully placed on his head. This was contrary to what Thomas and his jurymen would have expected in a victim of hanging. They reasoned that even a man intent on taking his own life would, at the very last, be unable to hold his body's reactive death spasms in check. Why, they puzzled, was Richard so unusually neat and tidy?

Thomas also observed that Richard's eyes and mouth were closed, 'without any staring, gapying, or frownyng'. Hanging is not a peaceful death, and in the majority of cases of death by hanging, both the eyes and mouth would be partially or completely open. Thomas would also have expected to have seen Richard's tongue protruding from his mouth; however this symptom was not present. There was a distinct lack of any drooling or 'spurgying' from any part of Richard's body, save for a few small drops of blood coming from his nostrils. Thomas particularly noticed that Richard had not dribbled any saliva, which is a very common symptom in cases of hanging. He also did not observe any urinary or faecal incontinence or any signs of seminal discharge. Thomas and his jurymen would have been well aware that during and after death by hanging victims were highly likely to void some form of bodily fluid. Save for the blood that had flowed from his nostrils, Richard's body was otherwise remarkably clean.

Next, the members of the inquest conducted a visual examination of the crime scene and noted three items of significance. The first related to how Richard could have positioned himself to tie the silk girdle to the iron hook. The length of the ligature from his neck to the hook was extremely short. If Richard had killed himself, then in order to reach the hook he would have had to stand on an object or item of furniture. The only usable item in the cell was a stool that was lying on top of the bed, some distance away from the body. There was nothing else nearby that Richard could have used to reach the hook. The second item of significance noted by Thomas was a half-melted wax candle that was about seven or eight feet away from Richard's body. Richard could not have snuffed out the candle from where he died, and it was highly unlikely that he had killed himself in pitch-darkness, especially when some finesse would have been necessary to get into an elevated position to secure the ligature. Lastly, Thomas noted that a mysterious mulberry-silk cloak, which a witness had reported seeing when Richard's body was first discovered, had disappeared. Whose cloak was it? Who had removed it, and why?

Once the initial visual examination of the scene was complete Thomas ordered his jury to take down Richard's body. As they began to lift the corpse, they were surprised to discover that the end of the silk girdle attached to the iron hook became loose and fell away. It was not securely tied, but was instead 'double cast' and held in place by a length of heavy chain. It seemed that the girdle had been thrown over the hook from below and heaved upon to pull the body up: a feat that would have been impossible for Richard to accomplish by himself. Once the body had been taken down the jury could examine it more closely. They observed that the ligature about Richard's neck was tightly tied and that the loop was too small for him to put his head through. The ligature was not a pre-fashioned noose that could slide closed; it had been tightly tied round Richard's neck. The knot was secured below Richard's left ear, causing his head to lean towards his right shoulder. This in itself was not indicative of anything untoward. One might assume that a person committing suicide would situate the knot at the back of their neck; however, knots are frequently found at the side and even at the front of the throat, and any coroner experienced in cases of genuine suicidal hanging would have been aware of this. As Thomas removed the silk girdle he noted the absence of any telltale ligature marks round the neck. A thinner or harder ligature, such as rope, cord or string, would leave a clear mark or furrow in the skin; however, given that the silk girdle was very soft, and possibly of a wide girth, it did not leave any marks.

Richard's neck had been broken, and there was a wound in one area where the skin had been 'fret and fallen away'. This wound was distinct from a ligature mark, and Thomas believed that Richard had been hit with an unknown object. He did not think it likely that Richard's neck had been broken by the ligature since the short drop of the ligature from hook to neck was not sufficient to cause a break. Fractures of the cervical spine are rare in routine cases of suicidal hanging. These kinds of injuries are, however, indicative of foul play. Even more damning was the fact that Richard's hands 'were wrung in the wrist', which Thomas took to be evidence that at some point prior to death Richard's hands had been bound. Victims intent on suicide might tie their own hands to ensure that they are unable to save themselves, however the bindings would

still be on the body after death. In Richard's case the bindings had been removed and were nowhere to be seen.

It was becoming increasingly obvious to Thomas that he
was not dealing with a case of *felo de se* but was instead
confronted with a murder staged as a suicide. The body
had none of the symptoms typical in hanging deaths and
it had evidently been interfered with. Evidence had been
removed from the scene, and most damning of all was the
simple fact that it was impossible for Richard to have pulled
his own body up on to the hook. The scene appeared to
be a poor attempt to hoodwink a coroner, but perhaps the
perpetrator did not expect the coroner to look quite so
closely. Thomas was convinced that Richard was innocent
of the charge of self-murder, and he refocused his investigation to discover the true cause of death and to seek out
the murderer or murderers.

Returning once more to the small quantity of blood
flowing from Richard's nostrils, Thomas noted that there
was no blood on the rest of his face, lips, chin, doublet,
collar or shirt. However, on the left side of his outer jacket,
just below the breast, there flowed 'greate streames of
bloude'. Two facts here were clear: Richard had haemor-
rhaged a good deal of blood from his nose, and somebody
had gone to some effort to clean it off his face. A 'cluster'
of blood was found underneath the downturned pocket-
flap of Richard's jacket, suggesting that the pocket-flap had

been turned up when he was haemorrhaging and turned down once he was dead. This rearrangement of Richard's clothing was probably done by the killer, who hoped to hide signs of violence on the body. The killer had washed Richard's face, combed his hair, and neatly set his hat upon his head. Thomas wrote in his report, 'it appeareth plainly to us all that the neck of Hunne was broken, and the great plenty of blood was shed before he was hanged'. This was puzzling, for given the quantity of blood that had been spilled over Richard's jacket there were no signs of that same blood on the floor where his body had been hanged. Surely the blood must have fallen and collected some-where? Thomas began searching the entire cell, and in a dark corner some distance away he found 'a great parcel of blood' on the floor. Thomas suspected that this was where Richard had been when his nose was bleeding, and this was where he had died.

The staged suicide had been amateurishly done, and after their investigation of the body and crime scene the jury unanimously agreed that 'Richard Hunne was murder'd'. But by whom? And why? The prime suspects were those select few men who had access to Richard's cell. The first was Dr Thomas Horsey, who was sneeringly called Thomas 'Heresie' by his enemies. He was chancellor to Bishop FitzJames and custodian of the Lollards' Tower. Richard may have been arrested under FitzJames's orders, but he was the direct prisoner of Dr Horsey. Witnesses suspected that Dr Horsey had planned to inflict terrible suffering upon his prisoner, as during one visit he had hurried up to Richard, fallen on his knees, held up his hands and prayed forgiveness, 'For all he had done to him, and must do to him.' How strange that a custodian of the tower, a man accustomed to the fates of suspected heretics, should give way to this emotional outburst. Whatever plans he had in mind for Richard must have weighed heavily upon his conscience.

The next suspect was the keeper of the jail and resident bell-ringer, John Spaldyng, who was reportedly a simple-witted man in possession of a small mind and a big mouth. Spaldyng held the only set of keys to Richard's cell and he had been acting suspiciously in the days leading up to the murder. A witness had come forward to relate an incident that had occurred a few days before Richard's death. He had seen Spaldyng in passing and made some enquiries after Richard's health. 'There is ordained for him so grievous penance,' Spaldyng had whispered in a conspiratorial fashion, 'that, when men hear of it, they shall have great marvel thereof.' Quite what he meant by this the witness did not say, but he clearly believed that dreadful punishment was due to his prisoner. The final suspect was Charles Joseph, a somewhat shady figure who was a summoner (one who delivered court summons, a most hated occupation), a drinker and a ladies' man. He was a known associate of Dr Horsey and had been seen leaving St Paul's early on Monday morning, just a few hours before Richard's body was discovered. His reputation as a brute for hire, and his presence so near to the crime scene mere hours after the victim had been killed, marked Joseph as deeply suspicious. Thomas was convinced that these three men were involved in the death of Richard Hunne, but could he prove it?

Believing themselves to be actors in a righteous cause, both Dr Horsey and John Spaldyng were seemingly unmoved by the death of an alleged heretic in their custody. They had the sense to keep their heads down and their mouths shut as they carried on with their day-to-day duties as though nothing were amiss. Charles Joseph, on the other hand, was not so composed, nor so clever. After he was seen leaving St Paul's early on Monday morning he hastened to the Bell tavern at Shoreditch where his horse was stabled. He was dressed for travel in a garish orange cloak and spurs and rode hard to his home, which was situated just outside London. Exhausted, cold and in a panic he pushed inside his house, where was greeted by his maid, Julian Little. The surprised maid noticed that her master was deeply disturbed and that he seemed to be in a hurry to unburden his conscience. She begged to know what was the matter, to which he replied, 'Julian, if thou wilt be sworn to keep my counsel, I will show thee my mind.' Seeing that her master was serious, she went off to fetch a Bible, placed her hand upon it and swore on oath to keep his secret. Satisfied by Little's apparent sincerity, Joseph confessed:

'I have destroyed Richard Hunne!'

'Alas master, how?' Little replied.

'I put a wire up his nose.'

Joseph was evidently remorseful, for he lamented to Little that he would gladly give 100 pounds if he could only take back what he had done, but alas, he wept to her, 'What is done cannot be undone.'

At the same time that Joseph was confessing his crimes to his maid, Thomas and his jurymen were on the hunt for Richard's killers. They had questioned witnesses and knew that Joseph had been seen leaving St Paul's that morning; they were keen to have Joseph brought before them so that they could interrogate him. Sensing that the net was drawing in around him, and fearing that he had made a gross error of judgement by trusting his maid, Joseph took flight. He went on the run and remained at large for over two weeks. Lacking both the means and connections to ensure a successful escape from justice, Joseph finally resurfaced on 22 December in the town of Good Easter in Essex, where he took sanctuary at the church of St Andrew's. He was soon afterwards removed from sanctuary and taken to the Tower of London for questioning. There he made a full confession in which he accused both Dr Horsey and John Spaldyng as his accomplices in murder.

He said that on the night of Richard's death all three of them climbed the stairs of the Lollards' Tower and went into his cell, where they found Richard lying on his bed. Dr Horsey had then cried out 'Seize the thief!', whereupon they fell upon the sleep-dazed prisoner and 'all murder'd him'. After these few words were said Joseph refused to go into any further detail as to how Richard was murdered; he didn't mention the wire, nor the fact that Richard's neck had been broken. He did, however, describe what they had done with Richard's body after they had killed him. He said that the three of them 'put the girdle about the prisoner's neck', and then he and Spaldyng had bodily heaved Richard up while Dr Horsey looped the other end of the girdle through the iron hook. Then, pulling with all their weight on the length of silk, they hauled Richard up as though he were on a pulley and 'hang'd him'.

Richard's death was a scandal that generated a great deal of gossip and argument throughout the country. Some were convinced that the Church had murdered an enemy in cold blood; others insisted that Richard had simply killed himself. Thomas More, a staunch Catholic and devoted heretic hunter, defended the Church, arguing that no murder had been committed. Richard Hunne, he scoffed, had been no more than an unrepentant sinner who had killed himself rather than submit to the humiliation of public penance. Others opined that Richard was puffed up by his own inflated sense of pride, and that he would have preferred death to the ignominy of continuing to live a shameful life. Countering this view was the Protestant martyrologist John Foxe, who said it was plain for all to see that Bishop FitzJames had given the order for Richard to be brutally slain in his cell. This murder, he maintained, was revenge against Richard for the legal suits he had brought against the Church. The famous chronicler Thomas Wriothesley wrote that Richard had been 'made an heretique for suinge a Praemunire' and that he had been killed because he refused to confess to heresy.

There was another theory, one preferred by many modern historians, which held that Richard's death was the accidental result of botched torture. Richard was, after all, a suspected heretic and he had steadfastly been withholding valuable information from the Church authorities. His Lollard sympathies were well known, and some suggested that his protracted and prohibitively expensive legal battles against the Church had been backed by wealthy Lollards in London's merchant community. Richard was no small fry, and it would have been a great victory for the Church to wring the names of his confederates from him. By destroying Richard the Church would not only be ridding the world of a much-hated heretic, it would also be freeing itself from the bother of litigation; Richard had long been a persistent thorn in its side and his downfall had become a matter of some urgency. Yet the evidence against Richard was weak and the Church was worried that he would soon slip out of its clutches. Time was running out and Bishop FitzJames desperately needed to wring a confession out of his prisoner before it was too late.

Since Richard had not been cooperating under conventional forms of interrogation, the Church was authorised under canon law to put him to torture. Modern imaginations might conjure up ghastly scenes of wild, unrestrained maltreatment subject to the bloodthirsty fantasies of degenerate men intent on letting all their inhibitions loose. Yet in truth torture was regulated by strict legal codes, bureaucracy and red tape. Under canon law torture was permissible so long as the torturers stopped short of 'bleeding the body', causing permanent injury or risking death. Restricted forms of torture were intended to allow members of the clergy to inflict pain upon a fellow human being without going so far as to cause death, which would be dangerous indeed for the torturer's soul. They were rules designed to protect the torturer, not the torturee. The Church had to be certain that in sanctioning torture it was operating within certain spiritual and ethical guidelines, although in reality those guidelines were frequently stretched to breaking point. Torturers were free to inflict whatever cruelties they could conceive of so long as they did not exceed the limits of canon law. This allowed them to invent a catalogue of imaginative, and utterly ghastly, horrors that they could inflict upon their victims while being assured of their own spiritual purity.

An example of Church-sanctioned torture can be found in the 1545 case of the suspected heretic Anne Askew. She was subjected to 'examination' on two separate occasions by the Bishop of London's chancellor. During her ordeal she was put to the rack until the sinews and ligaments in her arms and legs were torn, her shoulders and knees dislocated and her hip joints ripped from their sockets. She fainted repeatedly and was revived each time so she could be conscious to feel every turn of the rack's wheel. Between these sessions of torture she was dragged to the floor, where she lay in a dazed stupor as Church officials kneeled over her, whispering softly and trying in vain to coax from her numb lips the names of her fellow heretics. So brutal was her ordeal that she had to be carried in a chair to be burned at the stake. This was the 'gentler' kind of torture that was permissible for members of the clergy to perform upon suspected heretics. As Richard sat in his cold cell, surrounded by instruments of torture, he must have feared that he too would be subjected to a similar fate.

Historians theorising as to the events of Richard's murder

present a fascinating albeit bloodthirsty tale. In the days prior to his torture, and in accordance with canon law, Richard was fasted. FitzJames commanded 'that the prisoner should have but one meal's meat of the day', that meal being a single serving of meat at lunchtime, and no other food thereafter. On Sunday, 3 December, the day Richard was scheduled to be tortured, Charles Joseph rode into London and left his horse at the Bell inn at Shoreditch, with the order that it was to remain saddled and ready to go at a moment's notice. Whatever he had planned for that day, he made sure he had a swift getaway stationed nearby. Joseph walked to St Paul's, where he met with Dr Horsey and John Spaldyng. At about midnight they ascended the tower and quietly entered Richard's cell. There they saw him fast asleep on his bed, dressed in his jacket to ward against the bitterly cold December night. On Dr Horsey's command Joseph and Spaldyng dragged the prisoner from his bed and tied his wrists together with a ligature that was thin enough to cause wounding when he struggled. Fasted, trussed and half dazed, Richard was ready to be interrogated once more.

Dr Horsey intended to inflict violence upon his prisoner, yet he had been unwilling to dirty his own hands. Joseph had been recruited as a torturer, but in truth he was no more than a common thug; he did not have the skills or the stomach of a skilled inquisitor. Under the direction of

Dr Horsey, Joseph had attempted to insert a wire into Richard's nose. This was a common tactic from the torturers' handbook, for a wire up the nose, especially a wire that had been heated in a nearby candle flame, would cause immense suffering without leaving any incriminating marks. To perform this delicate act of torture Joseph would have had to restrain Richard, as no man or woman alive would sit quietly and endure so much without thrashing their head from side to side. It may have been now that the silk girdle first came into play; the soft material tied round Richard's forehead would have effectively restrained him without causing any undue damage. This was the moment when Joseph blundered by inserting the wire too far into Richard's nose, inadvertently piercing the cribriform plate separating the nasal cavity from the brain and thereby causing a possible brain injury and fatal haemorrhaging. Posterior bleeds caused by injury far back in the nasal cavity would have resulted in bleeding from both nostrils, as was observed by Thomas during his inquest

The profusion of so much blood flowing over Richard's face and down the front of his jacket must have been an alarming sight for the hapless inquisitors who, under the dictates of canon law, were prohibited from shedding even a single drop of their prisoner's blood. Joseph's blunder with a hot wire was quickly unfolding into a complete disaster. By then Richard must have been struggling with

the full force of a man driven wild by agony and the instinc-
tive need to preserve his own life. Violence ensued, and at
some point Richard received a powerful blow to his neck.
Perhaps somebody hit him with an object, as Thomas
suspected, or during the fray he fell and broke his neck on
the stocks. By some foul means Richard eventually lay on
the floor in the corner of his cell, where he continued to
haemorrhage a large quantity of blood before finally
succumbing to death. Dr Horsey and his dim-witted
confederates looked down at Richard's body in disbelief as
the reality of their situation came crashing in on them.
They had inadvertently and illegally killed their prisoner.

They had no choice but to try and salvage the situation.
If they could pass Richard's death off as a suicide then
maybe they could escape a murder charge. They had to
conceal any trace of violence and so they tidied up their
victim and wiped away his blood to hide the obvious nasal
haemorrhaging. Joseph then tied the silk girdle round
Richard's neck and between them they hauled his body
into a hanging position. It is strange they went to the
trouble of combing Richard's hair and placing his hat on
his head. Were these hapless killers simply overdoing
things as they primped and tidied their staged crime scene,
or was there more to their careful dressing of Richard's
corpse? Joseph had confessed to his maid that he felt a
great deal of regret for what he had done, and perhaps in

tidying Richard's body he was in some small way acting out his contrition. He had much to feel guilty for: by botching the torture he had not only taken Richard's life, but he had conspired to frame him as a felon whose suspected crime would have seen his body desecrated and denied Christian burial. As a theory this version of events is certainly compelling, and accounts for many of the strange inconsistencies observed by the coroner. However, outside of the scant testimonies given by the suspects we can never know for certain the exact details of the crime.

As the inquest progressed, FitzJames was becoming increasingly concerned. If the coroner indicted Dr Horsey and his underlings for murder, then all eyes would inevitably fall upon FitzJames as the man who gave the order. Both his reputation and that of the Church were at risk, and nothing short of drastic steps could put a stop to Thomas Barnwell and his troublesome investigation. Never one to shy away from extreme measures, FitzJames concocted a scheme that was as reckless as it was audacious. He seized custody of Richard's corpse with the intention of putting it on trial to answer charges of heresy. It was hoped that the business of a mysterious death in the Lollards' Tower would be buried in the excitement of a heresy trial, and Richard's status as a wronged innocent destroyed by a guilty verdict.

On Monday, 11 December Richard's corpse was put on trial in the Lady Chapel at St Paul's. The trial was presided over by Bishop FitzJames himself, and he was assisted by the Archbishop of York, Thomas Wolsey, and the Bishops of Durham and Lincoln. The chapel was packed with public notaries, doctors, abbots, priors and priests, along with 'a great rable' of other common anointed members of the Church. Thomas More was also present, and he watched the proceedings with the hawkish eye of a man fanatically devoted to the eradication of heresy. At the centre of all this noisome activity sat the silent corpse of Richard Hunne. His macabre presence in the chapel charged the atmosphere with an air of unprecedented strangeness. Never had such an extraordinary spectacle been witnessed before the ordinary Church court. A dead body had not been tried for heresy before, and many present that day shifted uncomfortably in their seats as they suspected that the proceedings may not be entirely legal. To make matters worse, it been a week since Richard's death, and while decomposition would have been slowed by the cold of the season he nonetheless would have been a grim and decidedly smelly defendant.

Richard's wretched corpse sat propped up as the charges against him were read out to the court, the most damning of which was his alleged possession of a Wycliffe Bible in English, complete with its famously heretical prologue. The Wycliffe Bible was a contentious item of evidence: since FitzJames had failed to mention it during the interrogation of his prisoner at Fulham, many believed it had been fabricated after Richard's death to ensure a guilty verdict. Luckily for FitzJames, the defendant was dead; he could make no reply and offer no defence to the flimsy charges made against him. Once the charges had been read the court was then asked if there were any who would speak on Richard's behalf; however none came forward. Over the course of a week the trial dragged on, with various witnesses sworn in to testify against Richard's steadily decomposing body. This dramatic farce was unnecessary as the outcome of the trial was a foregone conclusion. On 16 December Richard's corpse was found guilty of heresy and on 20 December it was taken to Smithfield to be burned at the stake.

What would the burning of a dead heretic have been like? For maximum impact, and to give an air of legitimacy to the sentence, it would have been conducted in much the same manner as the burning of living heretics, with some adjustments made to accommodate Richard's deceased state. His corpse would have been handed over to the secular arm of the law, as the Church did not sully its hands by conducting executions. Richard would have been stripped of any clothes he was wearing and dressed in a simple robe. A living heretic would have been paraded through the streets with a faggot of sticks upon his or her back, however Richard would most likely have been dragged through the streets behind a horse, or thrown into the bed of a cart to be driven from St Paul's to Smithfield. Once at Smithfield his body would have been chained to a large post, and bundles of wood stacked about him. Young green wood burned the slowest, and was often used to prolong the agonies of living heretics. There are accounts of condemned men and women taking upwards of forty-five minutes to succumb to the flames, and at all times they were conscious and amazed by the smouldering of their own limbs. It must have been a blessing for Richard's family to know that he had, at the very least, been spared this suffering.

Thomas Barnwell was enraged that the corpse under his jurisdiction has been snatched away, tried, condemned and burned while his inquest was still open. This outrageous display of power by the Church was intended to intimidate the coroner and bring to a grinding halt any further investigation into Richard's death. Yet, to FitzJames's dismay, his sham trial only served to galvanise the coroner and his jurymen, who threw themselves into their inquest with a vigour that was motivated by a desire to see justice done. Thomas was not afraid to push back and he refused to be silenced by the underhand tactics of powerful men in high places. He continued to track down and question witnesses and at the end of February 1515, the inquest at last reached its verdict: 'We find by God and all our consciences, that Richard Hunne was murdered. Also, we acquit the said Richard Hunne of his own death.' The inquest then went on to indict Dr Thomas Horsey, Charles Joseph and John Spaldyng for murder, stating that they had 'strangled and smothered' Hunne and 'feloniously slew him, and murdered him'.

Upon hearing this verdict FitzJames flew into a rage. In spite of his best efforts he had been unable to halt the outcome of the coroner's inquest, so now he did all in his power to ensure that legal proceedings could not go ahead. He wrote a furious letter to Archbishop Wolsey cursing Thomas's jury as 'false perjured caitiffs' who were determined to forsake their oaths. Wolsey was a powerful man whose star was rising, and he was able to use his position on the king's privy council to escalate the matter to the highest possible level. The king perceived a storm brewing and he hoped to calm matters by calling for a series of conferences to discuss clerical privilege and the jurisdictional boundaries of the Church courts. The Church maintained that Richard was a condemned heretic, and since his body had been properly assigned to the flames there should be nothing else to answer for. Thomas and his jurymen argued that a murder had been done and those men accused of that crime must be tried in the common law courts. The Church, they insisted, must not abuse its power and must not stand in the way of justice.

Thomas and his jurymen were dragged before the king's privy council, chief judges and justices of the realm and were strongly advised to reconsider their verdict. This must have been an intimidating and humiliating experience, and the privy council members did all in their power to undermine the coroner's inquest. On one occasion the jurymen's limited experience with hanging bodies was openly laughed at, and on another a witness who had given evidence at the inquest was mercilessly mocked as a fool. Yet in spite of these bullish tactics the jury would not be moved; to a man they held fast to their conviction that Richard had been murdered and they maintained that the three men indicted for that crime must be tried in the common law Court of the King's Bench. The king was forced to reach a compromise, although it was one that left both sides feeling decidedly bitter. He decreed that the indicted men would be tried in the Court of the King's Bench; however, the attorney general was instructed to accept the plea of not guilty. The case was dismissed, and Dr Horsey, Charles Joseph and John Spaldyng were free to go.

The general public resented the fact that the men indicted for the murder of Richard Hunne were excused from standing trial for their alleged crimes. How was it that members of the clergy could, with impunity, accuse good men of heresy and murder them without trial? The whole affair had started with a row over a christening gown, yet the underlying conflict had always been that of common people resenting the power and corruption of the Church. Bishop FitzJames had acted with the hubris of a man who believed himself to be untouchable. Yet in just a few short years the powerful tide of the Protestant Reformation was to sweep throughout Europe and men such as FitzJames would be stripped of the power and privilege of papal authority. In contrast to the cowardly actions of Bishop FitzJames, the coroner, Thomas Barnwell, had conducted himself with skill and determination. Throughout his inquest he demonstrated an impressive, albeit rudimentary, knowledge of forensic pathology and crime scene analysis that was grounded in years of practical experience working with the dead.

The members of his inquest were not rich or important men, they were simply tradesmen, shopkeepers, merchants and clerks. Yet they behaved with an astonishing amount of bravery. The inquest was a gruelling process that lasted several months, and throughout Thomas and his jury had been put under a great deal of pressure to drop the case and reach a verdict of *felo de se*. That they did not do so was a testament to their courage and civic values. They were up against some of the most powerful men of the realm, and while they may have been intimidated they never once faltered in their quest for truth. Richard may not have found justice through the court of the common law, however it is thanks to the coroner and his inquest that his innocence and victimhood were brought to light and made known to all who came to learn about the murder committed in the Lollards' Tower.

THE HONOURABLE
DROWNING OF
JOHN TEMPLE

On 5 November 1688 a vast invasion force led by the Protestant William of Orange landed at Brixham on Tor Bay. This foreign war fleet, consisting of fifty-three warships and 400 auxiliary vessels, was four times larger than the Spanish armada that had threatened England 100 years earlier. Mustered within those ships was an army of 40,000 men, of whom 21,000 were trained foot soldiers and 5,000 cavalry. As these forces disembarked and began the slow march to London they were met by cheers and cries of relief. Unlike the Spanish forces of Phillip II, this invading army had been invited by England's Protestant elite. They had urged William to overthrow the hated King James II, oust his Catholic progeny and restore England's monarchy to the one true Protestant faith. This so-called 'Glorious Revolution' was a blessedly bloodless affair. Without offering any resistance James fled to France, essentially abdicating his power and leaving the throne vacant.

On 11 April 1689 William and his wife Mary were jointly crowned as King and Queen of England, Scotland and Ireland. Their shared sovereignty spoke volumes as to the dilution of absolute authority. Gone were days of the divine right of kings and queens, when the monarch's word was law and none could defy their power. Under the newly minted Bill of Rights William's reign was restrained and his power was checked and balanced by Parliament. This was a new era, one of national importance but also one of individual ambition. Under the new regime men in positions of public office vied for advancement and dreamed of the honours they could reap through professional success. Some thrived in this cut-and-thrust world and some did not.

One such man who struggled to fit into the ruthless world of early modern politics was the enthusiastic yet ill-fated John Temple. He was an ambitious young man who, being barely out of his teens, envisioned before himself a long and respected career in politics. He was known to his many friends as a 'sedate and accomplished young gentleman' who seemed in his work to demonstrate a great deal of promise and natural ability. Some might have said that John's political ambitions were inherited from his father, Sir William Temple, who was himself an eminent statesman and political author. Poised at the beginning of his political career, John was keen to follow in his father's illustrious footsteps. Much rested on the young politician's shoulders, for out of the nine children born to Sir William, John was the only one to have survived into adulthood. Ten years previously his beloved sister Diana had died when she was fourteen, and none other of his siblings had lived beyond that age. Her death was hard on John, who not only had to contend with his own grief but also that of his parents who once more had to endure the hardship of losing yet another of their children. After Diana's death Sir William was reportedly 'wounded to the heart by grief' and 'quite sick' with melancholy. It was no small wonder then that Sir William's paternal attentions were so intensely focused on his one remaining child. As the sole surviving son John was painfully aware that the sum of his father's dynastic ambitions lay solely upon him.

Sir William was by all accounts 'a sound politician, a patriot and a great scholar', although these qualities were sometimes marred by touches of 'vanity and spleen'. His quick and deeply penetrating gaze belied a man of hard stoic principles and unrelenting ambition. On the whole John was keen to please his father, yet in one aspect of his life he flirted with disobedience. In spite of his father's enmity to the French ('a nation to whom Sir William ever bore a general hatred'), John married a Huguenot named Marie Duplessis-Rambouillet. She was an exceedingly wealthy woman of 'great piety and virtue' who bore John two healthy daughters. Regardless of Marie's good character, Sir William could scarcely stomach the admittance of a French woman into his English household. He sought to put a stop to any further such invasions by stipulating in his will that his granddaughters could only inherit the bulk of his estate on the condition that they never married Frenchmen. Such an episode demonstrated not only the depths of Sir William's xenophobia, but also his need to closely manage the lives of his family.

This controlling hand could be seen all the more clearly in the management of young John's political career. In 1684 Sir William arranged for his son to receive an official diploma of nobility which granted him entry to foreign courts, and shortly after that John was appointed as paymaster general. Sir William was a close friend of the newly crowned king, and he had no qualms about using that connection to push John further up the ladder of public office. On 12 April 1689, the day after the coronation, John was thrust on to the international stage as the newly appointed secretary of war. Sir William appeared to have full confidence in John's ability to execute the duties of his office, and at times he boasted of his son's prowess as a statesman. However, Sir William appeared to have been alone in esteeming the abilities of young John. It seemed that John struggled to keep up with his meteoric rise through the ranks of political power, as the duties placed upon him greatly outstripped his fledgling skill set. Tongues soon began to wag, and the gossips came out in force. John's position, they said, was no more than rank nepotism. Without his father he would be nothing, and in truth it was plain for all to see that he was wholly unsuited to the job. Nobody felt this censure as keenly as John did, for he feared that the gossips were right. He quailed at the measure of responsibility that had been heaped upon him, and suspected that it was only a matter of time before his critics were validated.

Nonetheless, John set out with his best foot forward and endeavoured to meet the lofty expectations of his father. His first week in office, however, was a complete disaster. The first matter of business thrust upon him was the rebellion in Ireland headed by the Earl of Tyrconnell. John had received a letter from Tyrconnell's secretary, Ellis, assuring him that his lord had promised to submit should the king offer favourable terms. Ellis urged John not to send any forces to Ireland, stating that to do so would not only scupper any hopes of negotiating peace, it would almost certainly bring war. Somewhat naively,

John took the word of his enemy at face value and did not consider for a moment that the letter may have been a trick designed to delay the arrival of English forces in Ireland. As secretary of war it would have behoved John to exercise caution and perhaps recall to mind the proverb that all's fair in love and war. Desperate above all things to avoid bloodshed, John not only rushed this letter directly to the king but also was at pains to praise Ellis as a trustworthy and honourable man.

With a sense of optimistic urgency, John then hastened to consult the friend of an old acquaintance, General Hamilton, who was at that time locked up in the Tower of London. He told Hamilton of his plan to hold off sending forces to Ireland so that he could instead offer terms of surrender to Tyrconnell. Hamilton, sensing that John was both utterly green and a soft touch, agreed that it was an excellent plan. Naturally Hamilton presented himself as the best man for the job, assuring John that as soon as he was freed from the Tower he would travel to Ireland, present the terms, and secure peace. Buoyed up by how smoothly things seemed to be going, John returned to the king to sing the praises of Hamilton. The king looked his secretary of war in the eye and asked him directly whether Hamilton could be trusted. With affluent praise and assurances as to the certainty of his intelligence, John convinced the king that Hamilton was an eminently trustworthy man who would deliver what he had promised. This was a grave error of judgement. The moment Hamilton set foot in Ireland he betrayed the king and swore his allegiance to Tyrconnell. Trusting in Hamilton was not John's only mistake; by following Ellis's advice to hold back English forces he had also given Tyrconnell ample time to muster troops and shore up his defences.

In the span of less than a week John had unwittingly wreaked irrevocable damage to public affairs, to the king's reputation and to his own honour. His intentions had been entirely good, for he wished more than anything to avoid unnecessary carnage. Yet by his 'hasty' and 'inconsiderate' actions many believed that he had assured both war and a greater loss of life: 'All ye blood shed in recovering Ireland', one critic hissed, 'wou'd call for vengence from him and his family.' John's peers mocked him for his incompetence, and wondered how one man could struggle with what was, reportedly, an easy position: 'The discharge of ye office of Secretaries of Warre', wrote the politician Christopher Hatton in a tone of some disbelief, 'is not a difficult taske.' The king and his Protestant allies had seized the throne without violence, and yet within a few days the inexperienced son of a famous politician had put that peace in jeopardy. Instead of upbraiding John for his folly, the king took pity on him and kindly expressed the opinion that 'Hamilton has not kept his word to us, but all men are not to be relied upon'. These conciliatory words did little to ease the shame of John's dishonour.

For many in early modern society the loss of honour was unendurable. Common wisdom held that fear of dishonour was greater than the fear of death or injury, and that 'an honourable death' was considered to be superior to a shameful life. Many of these views were grounded in the lingering codes of chivalry that still held fast in the imaginations of the elite classes. Highest among these chivalric virtues was that of familial honour, in particular the need to maintain a spotless reputation by upholding the glory of the family name. Such sentiments can be seen in a letter written by Sir Anthony Drury to his son William in 1620: 'to traduce my actions, stain my blood and dishonour my father, which is long since dead, are three mortal wounds to my soul which can never be cured'. Fathers worked hard to ensure that their sons proceeded with dignity and honour, and in turn sons strove to live up to their fathers' expectations.

These chivalric codes of familial honour were closely interwoven with the humanist principles of the time, which stressed the importance of civic duty and service to the commonwealth in the lives of all citizens. Those who succeeded in public office enjoyed a great deal of prestige, and it was the ambition of many fathers to see their sons prosper in that field. In promoting John into the office of secretary of war, Sir William had ensured that his son had the best possible start to his career. Yet he had also, unwittingly, set his son up to fail. John was simply too young and too inexperienced to succeed as the secretary of war, and the nature of his position ensured that his failure was played out on an international stage. It was a hard blow, for honour was not measured by individual perception; rather it was defined and magnified 'in the hearts and opinions of other men'. The greater the audience the greater the shame, and John Temple's disgrace was broadcast with relish throughout the whole of Europe.

Having blundered into public disgrace, John sought to salvage his reputation. He approached the king with the intention of resigning from his office, stating that 'he did not think himself qualify'd to discharge it with honour'. Yet to his horror the king denied him this gesture of atonement by flatly refusing to accept. 'Why, you are mad!' the king exclaimed, before lowering his voice to that of a tender father to advise, 'think better on't'. To John's further shame the king suggested that although he may not presently be up to the task of his office, he would surely grow into the role given two or three months. In the meantime he told John to relax and to allow his clerks to take care of business. The gesture was kindly meant, but it clearly implied that John's ineptitude was such that even mere clerks could do a better job. Not only had John been denied a chance to salvage his honour by resigning, he had been dealt a blow to his dignity by a king who coddled him like a child. Frustrated beyond measure, shamed before his father, pitied by his betters, reviled by his peers and forced to take a back seat in his own office, John could no longer endure the status quo of his circumstances. But what else could he do? When the peaceable means of erasing dishonour had been exhausted, young men living under the dictates of chivalric codes of honour were driven to seek more desperate, and more violent, conclusions to their shame.

In early modern society violence and honour were inexorably linked, especially among the gentrified classes. Perceived insult could be attached to the even the smallest acts of discourtesy: a withering look, the jostling of a shoulder in a crowded room or a sneering comment directed towards the fashion of man's hat might instigate acts of passionate and deadly violence. The riposte to insult by brawling and assault with deadly weapons was not uncommon, and duelling was frequently carried out by men who valued their reputations more than their lives. One man who seemed to revel in the dangers of honour-based violence was the courtier and politician George Villiers, the 2nd Duke of Buckingham. In December 1667, during a conference in the House of Lords, a fight broke out between Buckingham and the Marquess of Dorchester after they had exchanged some rude words. Buckingham, being the taller and sturdier of the two, loomed over Dorchester before snatching the periwig from the stupefied man's head. The subsequent brawl over this insult saw both men taken to the ground, where Dorchester in turn 'had much of the Duke's hair in his hand'. Another incident occurred the following year, in January 1668, when Buckingham was embroiled in an affair with the Countess of Shrewsbury. Unable to endure the shame of cuckoldry, the Earl of Shrewsbury called Buckingham out to a duel. Buckingham was only too pleased to accept, and in short order fatally shot the husband of his mistress. Rumour held that the countess, eager to watch the match, had disguised herself as a page and hidden among the gathered witnesses. Shortly after the duel Buckingham moved his mistress, 'the widow of his own creation', to live in his home alongside his wife. The general public did not bat an eyelid at the death of the earl, but were greatly scandalised by the impropriety of Buckingham's domestic arrangement.

Men of rank in early modern society were willing and ready to inflict violence and murder upon each other as a way of remedying the loss of personal honour. But what were men to do in situations in which they alone were responsible for their dishonour? Unable to lash out, they instead turned that violence inwards on themselves. Just as honour and inter-personal violence went hand in hand, so too did honour and suicide. To the early moderns the concept of an honourable suicide was extremely complex and contradictory. Self-murder was almost always universally reviled, and those found guilty of that crime were condemned by secular and religious authorities alike. Yet there were certain circumstances in which the slaying of oneself could be an ennobling act. Throughout history there were plenty of examples of honourable suicide. Humanist scholars cautiously admired the political suicide of Cato, who tore out his intestines rather than submit to Caesar's rule; students of ancient philosophy, men such as the stoic Sir William Temple, admired Socrates who, by drinking deadly hemlock, valued his moral excellence more than life; commentators on female virtue applauded Lucretia, who killed herself with a dagger in response to her rape; theologians and Protestant writers such as John Foxe praised the Marian martyrs, who willingly submitted to death at the stake rather than renounce their religious beliefs; and soldiers who threw themselves headlong into certain death were to be admired for their bravery.

The ambiguity surrounding deaths deliberately caused by reckless endangerment, as in battle, prompted a great deal of moral debate among those who sought to tease out a distinction between shameful suicide and honourable death. In his 1585 work *The Honourable Reputation of a Souldier*, the writer George Whetstone reported on the death of John Talbot, the Earl of Shrewsbury. During the

Battle of Castillon on 17 July 1453, the earl found himself confronted by a vast French force that greatly outnumbered his own. There was no chance of victory against such odds, and while the earl had the opportunity to retreat and wait for reinforcements he instead stubbornly held his ground. He turned to his son, Viscount Lisle, and said, 'Sonne, thou art yong, and mayst with thy honour flye: But I am old, and haue had my life honored with many victories, all which I should loose, if I should deferre my death . . . Therefore, I am bound to staye.' Lisle too chose to remain by his father's side, and in doing so knowingly submitted to certain death. Whetstone condemned the earl's actions and lamented that his sacrifice 'neither benefiteth his frend, nor hurteth his enimie', however he balanced his censure with admiration as he also wrote that 'the greatnes of these mens courages, are to be honored, although not necessary to be followed'. This was the paradox of suicide in the early modern imagination: it was understood to be a despicable crime, yet under the right circumstances it could also be a noble act.

The legendary suicides of men such as John Talbot echoed through the centuries and held a powerful sway over those who found themselves precariously torn between states of honour and disgrace. Honourable suicide was especially tempting to those in public office who had fallen from grace, for it not only afforded them an exit from their suffering but it gave them a chance to frame their deaths as acts of noble reparation. Just such a suicide was acted out by Dr Henry Butts, the master of Benet College and vice-chancellor of Queens' College, Cambridge on Easter Day in 1632. The years before his death saw him mired in crises and stress, for in 1630 the plague had struck. During this upheaval Dr Butts distinguished himself as a diligent manager of university affairs, yet the strain left him frayed and exhausted. He had also been deeply frustrated by a series of professional setbacks and scandals which threatened his ambition to a third term in office as vice-chancellor. Once the plague had burned itself out, and the threat of sickness had passed, life in Cambridge began to return to normal.

In late March 1632 King Charles and Queen Henrietta Maria, along with their court, had travelled from Newmarket to Cambridge where they planned to stay the night at Trinity College for feasting and entertainment in the form of a play. The choice of play, and who was to perform it, had been a point of contention between Dr Butts and the vice-chancellor of Trinity College, Dr Cumber. After a great deal of argument Dr Butts had his way, and that night the king and queen settled down to watch Butts's 'Queen's College English Comedy'. It was a complete disaster: the play lasted for almost seven hours and as it dragged on the audience groaned in frustration and wilted in their seats. Not only was it exceedingly boring, it also gave offence, with scenes featuring randy Puritans prancing about the stage like fools while fondling and kissing lusty harlots. Those who had been subjected to the dreadful ordeal described it as 'a long, dull, unseasoned piece of stuff' and an 'obscene, prophane, absurd and tedious comedy'. The king did little to disguise his distaste and the queen was deeply upset by the performance.

Dr Butts had become the laughing stock of Cambridge, and Dr Cumber was quick to subject him to a humiliating tongue-lashing in which he questioned both his judgement and his discretion. In the wake of this public telling-off Dr Butts visibly drooped, and 'his spirits being much dejected is falled sick'. His mood became sullen and his temper quick, and on one occasion he threatened to inflict violence upon his wife as she nagged him during dinner. Convinced that his professional ambitions were ruined, and unable to endure the ridicule of having presented such a ghastly play to the king and queen, Dr Butts announced to his friends and colleagues: 'I perceive all mine actions are misinterpreted, & yerefore I will go home & dye.' He first attempted to slay himself with a knife, but was foiled by the intervention of others. On 1 April, Easter Day, he had failed to turn up to Great St Mary's church where he was scheduled to preach a sermon. A search party was quickly dispatched to the master's lodge, where they discovered that Butts had hanged himself with a towel. The motive behind his suicide was clearly understood by his peers and that same day the politician and diarist William Whiteway wrote that Dr Butts had slain himself 'out of discontent, because the King shewed much dislike at a play'; a few days after that an anonymous letter writer opined that Dr Butts's suicide was the result of 'disgrace' and failed 'temporal hopes'. Butts had sought to erase his shame by underscoring this humiliating episode with a single, honourable act. By and large the response to his death was a mixture of sympathy and disgust.

Not all suicides committed in the name of honour were in and of themselves honourable. Some were viewed as being downright disgraceful, and others invited ridicule. The honour-based suicide of the parliamentarian and high sheriff of Essex, John Lemot Honywood, provided his enemies with ample material to heap shame upon his death. In 1693 Honywood's deceitful wife concocted a scheme whereby she convinced him that the entirety of his estate would be forfeit to the Crown unless he signed it over to her. This was of course a lie, and once her trickery was revealed Honywood flew into a rage that was stoked by the shame of being so easily deceived. Determined to end his life, he seized hold of a roast turkey, and by 'thrustinge the rump of [said] turkey down his throat' attempted to choke himself to death. When this failed he next tried to swallow the ends of tobacco pipes and throw himself down the stairs, but he was foiled in these attempts too. Giving his wife and her servants the slip, he at last managed to hang himself with a garter from a curtain rod. Public opinion held that Honywood's death was shamefully done. It was not only the motive that signified an honourable suicide but also the means. A soldier who bore his breast to enemy fire was to be praised, but a politician who tried to choke himself with a turkey drumstick was no more than an object of derision.

On the morning of Friday, 19 April, a week to the day that John had been appointed secretary of war, the young politician resolved to kill himself. He spent the morning in his office at Whitehall, where he diligently worked on some small matters of business alongside his two clerks. At about midday he left work and made some enquiries into the tide times for that day. After this he walked to the river to hail a wherry-boat (today's water taxi) from Whitehall Stairs, which descended into the water. The streets of London were winding, narrow and constricted by trade and traffic, and the only crossing connecting citizens to the north and south banks was London Bridge. If one wished to travel with ease across London, it had to be by water. Wherries were small, light boats that could carry up to five passengers and were frighteningly slim, measuring six yards in length and a scant one yard wide. The wherrymen who skilfully steered those boats jostled about the stairs lining the river, vying for custom and lustily crying out 'Oars! Oars!' in the rough brogue unique to their class. London's wherrymen were a proud group of tradesmen who passed the mysteries of their profession down generations of river-dwelling families. It was no mean feat to navigate the Thames's strong and dangerous tides, and they jealously guarded their knowledge alongside their exclusive rights as London's ferrymen. Looking out over the water, one would have been impressed by the vast number of wherries carrying passengers and goods. John Stow's 1598 *Survey of London* estimated that at least 2,000 wherry-boats and 3,000 wherrymen were working the river at a time. Just over ninety-years after Stow had made his calculations, as John tentatively stepped into one such wherry-boat, that number would have been even greater.

John instructed the wherryman to take him downriver, and about halfway between Whitehall and London Bridge he asked to be put ashore. He entered a house and there made up some packages and letters of business that were to be put into the hands of some Dutch colleagues who were due to travel to Scotland the following day. Next he sealed more packages and placed them in the hands of a porter. Having discharged these last duties of his office, John considered himself free to withdraw from his life. As he walked back to the Thames it was about five or six o'clock in the evening, and the ebb tide was at its peak. He descended the Old Swan Stairs and deliberately hired a wherryman who was unknown to him, for what he had planned he did not wish to impose upon even the slightest of his acquaintances. Once the wherryman had pushed off John told him to head downriver towards Greenwich and to 'shoot the bridge' through the centre archway of London Bridge.

Shooting the bridge was a dangerous business that only the bravest and most skilled watermen were able to perform. London Bridge was a mighty structure, built to withstand the powerful tides that dragged beneath its arches. Unlike today, the bridge in the seventeenth century was teeming with commercial and residential properties. Weatherboarded timber shops with lead-latticed window fronts loomed up to five storeys high. Many of these properties were joined over the roadway by the 'cross building' of their upper storeys, turning the road below into a gloomy passageway. These tightly clustered rows of shops perched upon hammer beams that extended some twelve feet out over the frightful roaring of the river below. From a vantage point on the river the entire length of London Bridge seemed to sag with the overhang of timber-framed houses, hanging-cellars (small storage rooms suspended over the water) and sprawling beams. Constant maintenance was necessary to hold back the damage wrought daily by the powerful tides that swept below the bridge. Protective islands called 'starlings' had been built round the arches to channel and control the river's flow, effectively turning London Bridge into a dam.

During certain tides the difference in water level on either side of the bridge could be as much as five feet. At these times the water roaring through the arches was deadly rapids that flowed with 'such violence and hideous noyse' that it 'affrighted' and 'astonished' even the most seasoned of wherrymen. John had timed his journey to coincide with the height of ebb tide, and he had instructed his wherryman to go through the central arch where the rapids were at their most fierce and dangerous.

The small boat plunged into the violent rapids and was dragged at a terrifying speed through the archway. The brave wherryman strained to keep his boat stable as he steered it away from the starlings, upon which his small craft could be smashed to pieces. Over the mighty noise of the river he shouted to his passenger to hold fast. At that precise moment John calmly placed a single shilling and his hat upon the narrow seat, and then stood up. He said a few words, which were lost to the roaring sound of the rapids, before he was pitched into the raging water. The horrified wherryman cried out, and heaved on his oars in a desperate effort to reach his lost passenger. Through the foam and spray of the rapids he saw John rise once, and then again above the waterline before his body sank out of view. There was nothing the wherryman could do save to stare helplessly behind him as his boat raced away from the drowning man in his wake. As soon as he was able, the wherryman sculled to the shoreline and through chattering teeth called to his fellow watermen for aid. He could not tell whether his passenger had fallen in by accident, or if he had deliberately cast himself into the rapids. Once the initial surge of panic had calmed, the wherryman thought to conduct a search of his boat. There on the seat he found a shilling, left as payment for the journey, and a note written in pencil upon a hat. The note read:

My folly in undertaking what I was not able to perform, has done the King and the Kingdom a great deal of prejudice: I wish him all Happiness, and abler servants than John Temple.

Was this a suicide note? Or simply the private jottings of a man overwhelmed by his inadequacies? At that precise moment no one could say for certain. Word of the accident quickly spread through town. Before long several of John's friends heard what had happened and raced to the waterside to see what could be done. Upon learning that John had not been found, they rallied to offer a reward to any man who was able to recover his body. Motivated by this financial incentive, and perhaps in no small part by morbid curiosity, men in boats dragged the river with ropes and grapples. The search continued for several days, during which the king was growing increasingly worried as to the whereabouts of his secretary of war. At last, on 22 April, one lucky boatman was dragging a ballast-hole close to the Pickle-Herring Stairs, near the Tower of London, when his grapple snagged in the pocket of John Temple's coat. The waterman heaved the corpse ashore and hailed nearby searchers to alert them of his discovery. The condition of the body must have been a terrible sight, for a corpse submerged in water for so many days would have borne signs of bloating, swelling and decomposition as well as abrasions and trauma from the rough currents that drove it into the ballast-hole. Yet despite these disfigurements the body was quickly identified as John Temple and carried to the water bailiff's house near the Fishmongers' Hall, where it was placed in a lined coffin and covered with a lace shawl to await the arrival of the coroner.

During the inquest the coroner and his jurymen debated whether the cause of death had been misadventure or self-murder. Upon first view of the body the inquest noted that John was very richly dressed, having on his person an expensive watch and other items of considerable value such as a beautiful silver-hilted sword that he wore at his side. His manner of dress excited speculation. Some wondered why a man intent on throwing himself into the river would bother with such finery, while others held the view that a gentleman was entitled to meet his end attired however he so pleased. Such musings were quickly put aside, however, when the coroner discovered that John's pockets had been filled with stones and sewn shut. This deliberate weighing down of his person was taken as evidence of John's intention to commit suicide. Further to their view of the body, the jury heard evidence concerning John's melancholic illness that had been occasioned by his recent failures as secretary of war. Sadly, the record of the inquest's verdict does not survive, however it was widely reported in pamphlets and newspapers that John had killed himself. Sir William could scarcely believe that his only surviving son was dead, and he would have been incapacitated by grief were it not for his strong stoic principles, without which he 'would certainly have sunk'.

The response to John's death revealed the contradictory way in which the early moderns thought about and interpreted suicide. Gossip mongers, newspaper men and pamphleteers had no doubt that John was a 'self-murderer', but the manner in which they reported his crime belied a largely sympathetic attitude. One publication wrote that this obvious suicide was a 'sad and lamentable' affair that was to be counted as an 'unhappy accident' rather than a malicious act. The politician and diarist Sir John Reresby wrote that the incident was 'a very sad accident', and the famed French journalist Guillaume de Lamberty reported that John's death was 'a particular misfortune' due to sadness and dishonour. Completely lacking in the surviving accounts of John's death was any hint of censure, anger or disgust that was typical in the reporting of suicides. Printed accounts typically held the act of self-murder to be 'barbarous', 'monstrous', 'unnatural' or 'ungodly'. Contrary to this, the language used to describe John's death was that of accident and misadventure.

The reasons for this kindly reportage could have been ascribed to John's social class, royal connection, profession, wealth, family, and even faith – yet there is no doubt that the motive and method of John's suicide also aroused the romantic imagination of a public that valued codes of honour and violence. De Lamberty speculated that John 'chose the manner of death which seemed to him the most reliable and the shortest'. Perhaps so, but wouldn't it have been quicker and easier for John to have slain himself in the privacy of his own chamber using a gun, knife or rope? Or, if he had wished to end his life by drowning, why did he not simply throw himself from London Bridge into the raging waters of the Thames below? By shooting the bridge during the height of ebb tide, and by standing so recklessly in the boat as it surged through the fastest parts of the rapids, John had placed himself in a situation whereby he did not kill himself, but instead allowed himself to be killed. This may seem an arbitrary distinction, yet it mattered. If a soldier such as the Earl of Shrewsbury could choose a foolish, careless yet honourable end by standing in the way of certain death, then so too could John Temple.

In life and death John's actions were driven by his honourable intentions. As a son he had wished to live up to the expectations of his famous father, to embody the hopes and ambitions lost through the deaths of nine children before him and perhaps in no small part to atone for his disappointing marriage. As a man he wished to succeed in his chosen profession and excel at the forefront of a new political age that had been ushered in by the Glorious Revolution and the coronation of a king and queen constrained by Parliament. Yet for all his enthusiasm John lacked experience and was hopelessly lost when confronted by his more worldly and more sophisticated enemies. In his pursuit of honour he had not only overreached himself, he had destroyed his reputation beyond all hope of repair. Frustrated in his attempts to make amends, and unable to unleash violence upon others as a means of restoring his honour, John had been left with no choice but to end his own life. It was, after all, far better for him to submit to an honourable death than it was to endure the misery of a shameful life. As he stood amid the Thames's raging rapids and allowed himself to be thrown overboard John staged his suicide to be a more akin to an act of reckless endangerment than deliberate self-murder. After the fact he had no power to dictate the public's response to his actions, and who could say if he would have been pleased or disappointed by the pitying words of sadness that followed his death. At the very least, he was remembered as an earnest and worthy man who, for good or ill, had acted with honour.

ACKNOWLEDGEMENTS

I wish to express my heartfelt gratitude to Dr Tom Roebuck, for without your wisdom and guidance over the years there would be no book. My thanks also to my friend Maja Bodenstein; you did so much to help me get this project off the ground and have always been on hand for a pep talk. To my husband Dave for your endless love and support, you believed in me every step of the way. Last but by no means least thank you Mum, Jo Dixon, you read my early drafts with so much enthusiasm and never doubted I could do it. It means a lot.